LIFE & OTHER
PASSING MOMENTS

Borgo Press Books by VICTOR J. BANIS

*The Astral: Till the Day I Die * Avalon: An Historical Novel * Charms, Spells, and Curses for the Millions * Color Him Gay: That Man from C.A.M.P. * The Curse of Bloodstone: A Gothic Novel of Terror * Darkwater: A Gothic Novel of Horror * The Daughters of Nightsong: An Historical Novel* (Nightsong Saga #2) * *The Devil's Dance: A Novel of Terror * Drag Thing; or, The Strange Tale of Jackle and Hyde * The Earth and All It Holds: An Historical Novel * A Family Affair: A Novel of Terror * Fatal Flowers: A Novel of Horror * Fire on the Moon: A Novel of Terror * The Gay Dogs: That Man from C.A.M.P. * The Gay Haunt * The Glass House: A Novel of Terror * The Glass Painting: A Gothic Tale of Horror * Goodbye, My Lover * The Greek Boy * The Green Rolling Hills: Writings from West Virginia* (editor) * *Green Willows: A Novel of Terror * Kenny's Back * Life & Other Passing Moments: A Collection of Short Writings * The Lion's Gate: A Novel of Terror * Love's Pawn: A Novel of Romance * Lucifer's Daughter: A Novel of Horror * Moon Garden: A Novel of Terror * Nightsong: An Historical Novel* (Nightsong Saga #1) * *The Pot Thickens: Recipes from Writers and Editors* (editor) * *San Antone: An Historical Novel * The Scent of Heather: A Novel of Terror * The Second House: A Novel of Terror * The Second Tijuana Bible Reader* (editor) * *Spine Intact, Some Creases: Remembrances of a Paperback Writer * Stranger at the Door: A Novel of Suspense * Sweet Tormented Love: A Novel of Romance * The Sword and the Rose: An Historical Novel * This Splendid Earth: An Historical Novel * The Tijuana Bible Reader* (editor) * *The WATERCRESS File: That Man from C.A.M.P. * A Westward Love: An Historical Romance * White Jade: A Novel of Terror * The Why Not * The Wine of the Heart: A Novel of Romance * The Wolves of Craywood: A Novel of Terror*

LIFE & OTHER PASSING MOMENTS

A COLLECTION OF SHORT WRITINGS

VICTOR J. BANIS

THE BORGO PRESS

MMXII

LIFE & OTHER PASSING MOMENTS

SECOND BORGO PRESS EDITION

Published by Wildside Press LLC

www.wildsidebooks.com

DEDICATION

Special thanks to Heather and Dave,
for all their efforts on my behalf;

And to John Betancourt, for bringing
so many of my books back to life.

CONTENTS

INTRODUCTION
THIRTY YEARS AMONG THE DEAD

I first heard the name "Victor Banis" some three decades ago, while I was working on the several volumes of a bibliography on *Science Fiction and Fantasy Literature* (Gale Research Co., 1979-92). He was apparently the real author behind "Jan Alexander" and "Lynn Benedict," two pseudonymous writers of a series of supernatural horror paperbacks published from 1970 on. And he was also, or so it seemed to me, one "Victor Jay," who'd penned a couple of raunchy, funny ghost stories in the late '60s and early '70s.

I hadn't read any of his books, although I acquired most of them for my collection of historical pbs—but I wondered occasionally who he was and what he'd done, and whether he was an old-time pulpster or a child of the paperback era.

Thirty years are a very long time. Three decades ago I was a not-yet-thirty editor and publisher and writer with unlimited energy and an unlimited event-horizon ahead of me. A millennium later I'm a not-yet-sixty editor and writer with limited energy and a much shorter way to go on the road of life.

Most of the writers and editors that I met or knew in my youth are gone now: Robert Nathan, Leonard Wibberley, Malcolm "Mac" Hulke, Jerome Bixby, and so many others from the fantasy and science fiction and mystery communities. They helped shape my career—and greatly enriched my life.

Victor Banis was not among them, however.

My brief sojourn in L.A. during 1969-70 may well have overlapped his own, but our *professional* circles did *not* intersect, save peripherally through my compilations and acquaintances. I continued thereafter to write and edit and eventually publish from San Bernardino, driving into L.A. several times a month during the 1970s—but I just never encountered the man, which was entirely my loss. And so it goes—and so it went—for the both of us during the ensuing decades. Thirty-plus years are a very long time indeed.

And then, just over a year ago, I encountered the elusive Banissimus once more, and that, my dear friends, is a story in and of itself.

A while back I was asked by my friend Bill Contento to update my old SF biblio on CD-ROM, and I'd started checking and rechecking the author information and bib data, a long, tedious, and as yet unfinished business. Lo and behold, I found a few more tomes by Mr. Banis to add to my growing list—but nothing published past 1980. Either the man was dead, or he'd completely stopped writing fantasy and horror (false syllogisms both, as it turned out).

Then in March 2006, I was approached by Wildside Press to edit a line of reprints for them, to be partially derived from the old Borgo Press list that Mary and I had published for a quarter century. I missed editing, so I agreed to participate.

But I was still working on that blankety-blank update to *SF&FL*, and while checking authors' names on the Internet, I was pulled to a website featuring the pseudonymous works of one William Maltese—including a number of SF titles already listed in my oversized reference tomes. I dropped him an e-note, and immediately got a response that helped clarify what he'd penned.

And in the course of our several conversations I began to wonder, oh yes I did, ladies and gents, whether or not I could expand my offerings at WP by reprinting *fiction* by Mr. Maltese—and possibly others. For it seemed to me that the market was ripe for such a revolution. And, wonder of wonders, my prescient publisher did agree.

And then William mentioned several friends of his—all longtime pros in the business—who might also be interested. There was Ms. X. There was Mr. Y. And there was Mr. Z—that damned name again: *BANIS! Victor J. Banis!*

After thirty years among the dead, the man had resurrected himself. He was living in the wilds of West Virginia (at which point I wondered if he was actually *brain*-dead, having encountered some of the rougher areas of that lovely state in my many meanderings!).

"No, no, no," the Maltese falcon chirped back at me, "he's living in a suburb of D.C. He'd be happy to hear from you. Just mention my name in Atlantis."

So I did—write him, that is—and did—hear back from him—and did eventually publish him, and did finally talk to him—and found a lovely person and a helluva good writer in the process—and, I hope, a lifelong friend.

You see, gentlefolks—there are writers, and then there are WRITERS. I ran that one in all-caps so that those of you are just dozing will sit up and take notice. Fra Reginaldo is about to make one of his official *pronunciamentos*: those of us who sling this shit professionally know the difference between the hacks and the hack-nots. We recognize the prose that sings, the words that bite, the verbs that grab. We wish those talents were ours— oh, we do so envy those penmen who make it look that easy. Because it's not that easy, people. In fact, it's not easy at all!

Read a passage from one of Victor's novels. Note the smoothness of the dialogue, the way the story flows, the rhythm of the language, the subtle, special touch of the master wordsmith as he paints his portraits in prose. It doesn't get much better than this.

So why isn't Victor Banis a household name?

If life were fair, the many talented writers that I've known would all have died rich and championed and well-read. Sadly, that's not the case, and there isn't any good reason for it. For every J. K. Rowling, there are ten thousand, a hundred thousand

Jerry Bixbys, who at the end of his life was staying alive by selling off pieces of his treasured art book collection.

There's a lesson in there somewhere, I suppose. The best way to support the writers you like is by buying their books, savoring their books, cherishing their books. The really top-notch writers are rare birds indeed, but their works merit rereading again and again.

Victor Banis is definitely a member of this exclusive club. You need go no further than the first paragraph in this new collection of tales and reminiscences to relish the magic of his pen. He sets the tone, grabs the eye, and rivets the reader right to the page. And he's funny—*ha, ha*, I mean, not peculiar—I swear that I've eaten at some of the places reviewed by The Underground Diner, including a houseboat restaurant run by a distant cousin of mine in Tennessee.

So, gentle readers, it's time to praise Caesar and to hail Caesar. He came, he saw, he conquered, but the "Victor"y—hey, it's all ours! In the words of the immortal Horace, Victor J. Banis has created a monument more enduring than brass—and a much more readable one too!

—Robert Reginald
San Bernardino, California
27 July 2007

PART ONE
LIFE & OTHER PASSING MOMENTS

THE BIRTHDAY BOY

She baked him a wheat cake, because that was his favorite. He'd have been happy with anything, of course, or even with nothing at all. The sweetest boy, everyone said so. Never a moment of trouble, never a word of complaint. What mother could ask for a more perfect son?

She had gotten him a new pair of shoes. It had taken her the entire year to save the money for them, and she had had to forego so much that the money could have provided for them; but this mattered, this was important—that they celebrate these young years of his, that each of the birthdays must be made special. It was all she could do. The poor are limited, but not in love, at least. She would do this, and if her husband thought her foolish, he did not say so, and for that she was grateful.

When the cake was ready, she went to where he was working in the shop with his father. He let the boy come in alone. This was her time, mother and son together. He understood. That was his gift. It was all he could give.

"How he has grown," the other women said, and did not know that their words were like a knife in her heart when they spoke them. He was a serious child, not given much to play or laughter, but when he smiled, as he did now, it was like the sun bursting through a bank of storm clouds. She could tell that he was delighted with the shoes, and the cake, which he especially loved. They ate it together, each crumb sticking painfully in her throat, but somehow, she managed to smile back at him, and if he guessed her pain, he did not remark on it, and only smiled more sweetly at her.

When the cake was gone, he put on the new shoes, and came to embrace her, and she had to fight the urge to cling to him, to hold him to her, because she knew that was foolish. You could not keep your boy a boy. No matter how tightly you held him, he would grow.

He kissed her brow and went out to show his new shoes, and she sat, the tears running freely now down her cheeks, her heart breaking within her. She did not look up when her husband came in.

He knelt on the dirt floor with her, and took her in his arms. His rough carpenter's hands were astonishingly gentle. "Ah, Mary," he said, wishing that he could take the pain away from her. "Don't cry, my darling."

"Oh, Joseph, Joseph," she sobbed against his chest, "Another year gone by."

He held her, and said nothing. What could he say? It had all been settled when the boy was born—those strange men, the lights—the time passed, and what would be, would be. He could not change any of it.

He could not help his heart aching, though, for the mother, knowing.

WELCOME TO ANTOINETTE'S

"You'll have to go now, Victor," the woman behind the counter said. "I've got to close up."

He had been staring at a print on the coffee house wall: a Thomas Kincaid inn, mullioned windows, pink and white flowers lining the walk, and an aproned woman smiling beatifically from the open doorway. "Welcome to Antoinette's," the plaque at the bottom said.

"Sure," he said, and drained the last of the long-cold coffee from the bottom of the paper cup, hoping maybe she would offer a free refill, but without much hope. She hadn't even charged him for the original fill.

He realized belatedly that she had called him by name. Did he know her? He glanced over to where she was busy filling a paper bag with rolls from the shelves. She looked familiar—but he was too hungry, and too tired. His memory had gone to sleep while he struggled to keep body awake.

"Here." She came from behind the counter and set the paper bag on the table in front of him. "It's the old rolls, they'll just throw them out when they open after Christmas. There's no point in their going to waste. And a panino someone forgot to pick up."

"Do I know you?" he asked.

"Well, you've been sitting here long enough, we could be old friends." She smiled. "It's Karen. Karen Delvecchio."

Which rang no bells in his benumbed mind. "Thanks," he

said, setting the bag on his lap, as if she might change her mind and try to take it back.

She saw him glance again at the print of Antoinette's. "Maybe you should be looking at that one instead," she said, indicating the print that hung near the register. He knew which one she meant. There was a birdhouse, in an intense blue, and in the foreground, a large brown bird, holding a glass bottle in his feet, and inside the bottle, what appeared to be a note. There were other bottles, too, floating in a stream at the bottom of the picture. "Heavenly Messages," it was titled.

"I don't get that one," he said, getting up and slipping into the light windbreaker, and donning the thick blue parka over that. The temperature outside had been hovering at about twenty degrees earlier; by now, it was probably more like zero. "I don't know what it means."

"Maybe *that's* what it means," she said. "Maybe Heavenly messages aren't supposed to be writ large, so we can take them in at a casual glance. Maybe we're supposed to have to work on them."

He shrugged. "Maybe. I like Antoinette's better, though. A cozy little restaurant. Warm food, a fire burning. Nothing to puzzle over." He started toward the front door.

"Wait, here," she said. She dipped her hand into the tip jar on the counter and pulled out a handful of bills, and thrust them at him.

"What's this?" he asked, staring stupidly at the money.

She gave him a pale smile. "Maybe it's one of Heaven's messages," she said. "Merry Christmas."

He knew he ought to say the same back to her, but the words wouldn't come. Merry Christmas? Nothing merry about it, that he could see.

"Goodnight," he said instead, and went out. He heard her lock the door after him, eager to go home, to spend the rest of Christmas Eve with her family. He couldn't blame her. It wasn't her fault he didn't have a home to go to, or a family to share it with. The sign said they closed at eight o'clock tonight, and it was after ten now. She had stayed late as it was, to let him nurse that free coffee, and put off the inevitable. He knew that he ought to be grateful, but the gratitude was sour in his mouth.

The inevitable was colder even than he had anticipated. It had begun to snow, and a devilish wind spit the snow in his face and seemed to slice right through the parka. He didn't have gloves, and it was too cold to carry the paper bag of rolls barehanded. He tucked it inside the parka, and looked at the bills she had handed him. All ones, eleven of them. He shoved them and his hands into his pockets, and thought, I could get something hot to eat, if anything's open. The Seven Eleven, maybe? Or, better yet, there were the tacky motels on the edge of town. Maybe he could persuade a night clerk to let him have a room for the night on the cheap. Hey, it was Christmas Eve, wasn't it, as everyone kept reminding him?

He veered off in the direction of Winchester, cutting through the deserted mall. The night was preternaturally still. The steakhouse next door was closed, and the Office Max across the street. Everything was closed; everyone was at home, or hurrying to get there in the lone car that suddenly loomed out of the darkness. On an impulse, he stuck out his thumb, but they whizzed by as if they hadn't seen him at all, the tires splashing wet snow across the tops of his shoes.

Not quite everyone was home, as it turned out. He saw someone sitting on the curb a few feet away, and slowed his steps. These days you had to be chary of strangers at night, even on Christmas Eve night. The bad guys didn't take holidays off.

It was an old man, though; he certainly did not look a threat. What he looked, was wracked with despair—and cold—he was in his shirtsleeves, despite the bitter cold.

Victor hesitated, thinking he would slip on by, hopefully unnoticed. But the slump in the old man's shoulders...and, when he got closer, he could hear that he was crying, great heaves that shook his body and sounded like the muffled wail of a coyote in the silent night.

"Are you okay?" Victor asked, coming closer.

"Okay? Now there's a laugh," the old man said without looking at him. "The damn bastards! They took everything. Took my coat, took the few pennies I had in my pocket, took my pint of Jack. Everything. And on Christmas Eve, too."

"You were mugged?"

"Three of them, their damned britches hanging halfway down their butts. Little punks. If I'd been twenty years younger...."

What could he say? He was no stranger himself to life's misfortunes. Still.... "What are you going to do?"

"Do? What can I do? Sit here and cuss, is all I can see."

"You'll freeze to death. It must be close to zero by now."

The old man did look at him then. He stared, stared in particular at the blue parka, as if judging its warmth. Victor felt its woolen bulk seem of a sudden to weigh heavily upon him. Automatically, he pulled it closer about himself, asserting his ownership. The old man saw the gesture, and shrugged, and put his head in his hands. There was blood on his cheek, apparently where someone had struck him.

Damn. "Here," Victor said aloud, unfastening the buttons with numb fingers. He slipped the coat off, and thrust it at the man. "Take this."

"Just means you'll freeze to death instead of me," the old man said, but he took the coat, and hurriedly slipped his arms into the sleeves.

"No, I've got this windbreaker, see, it's warmer than it looks, actually. And some other stuff under it, it's what they call layering. To be honest, I was thinking about taking the coat off, anyway, it was almost too warm."

The old man got the coat buttoned. He stood up, brushing snow of the seat of his pants. If he recognized the lies, he chose to ignore them.

"Glad to have it," he said.

"You could still freeze," Victor said.

"I know a place," was all he said. He started to walk, back the way Victor had come. He had gone about twenty feet before he looked back and said, "Merry Christmas." He disappeared into the darkness and the swirling snow.

Merry Christmas, again. Why did people say that, when there was so clearly nothing merry about it? You'd think they would choke on the words. You'd think that old guy in particular would choke trying to get them out.

He put his head down and began to walk again, in the opposite direction, shivering in the light windbreaker and cursing himself. What a damned fool thing to do. The old man was right, he would probably be the one now to freeze to death, unless he could make it to one of those motels, persuade somebody to make Christmas merry instead of just wishing it.

He plodded through the snow, the bag of food under his arm, hands deep in the pocket of his trousers, half frozen already, trying to think of things to distract himself.

He thought of his mother. What would she say now? He pictured her now, that little woman who had looked so frail, and been so tough. You had to be tough, to raise twelve children with an abusive husband and scarcely a penny to your name.

Lift one foot up, put it down, lift the other, that was how you got where you wanted to go. He remembered her saying that. He lifted his foot, counted: one, two, three....

He had his head down against the wind, so he almost didn't see the car, sitting half off the road, until the man swung the door open as he was passing, and said, "Excuse me, sir, I wonder if I could ask you something?"

Victor jumped, startled, and took a quick step backward, his foot sliding in the snow, so that he almost fell.

"What the hell?" he swore aloud, his arms windmilling to keep his balance.

"Sorry, I didn't mean to scare you," the stranger said. He was short, and thin, and needed a shave, and his clothes looked like he had been sleeping in them. "It's just, my family and me, we got stuck, we were on our way to my wife's family, for Christmas, only we run out of gas, and we got no money, and I was wondering if you could spare a dollar or two?"

Victor's fingers automatically clenched the wad of ones in his pocket. "No, I got nothing," he said. "Sorry."

"That's okay," the man said resignedly. "It's hard times, ain't it?" He turned back to the car, and then looked at Victor again. "You look powerful cold, in just that little jacket. Maybe you ought to sit here in the car with us for a spell. There's no heat, except from our bodies, but it's out of the wind, at least."

"No, I," Victor started to say, but a fierce gust of wind swept over him just then, seemed to go right through him. How far was it to those motels, anyway? A mile? Two miles. Maybe a rest would do him good.

"Yes," he said instead. "I'd be grateful."

"Glad to share what we can," the man said. He opened the back door for Victor to slide inside. A small boy sat in the far corner, eyeing him warily as he got in. The man got into the front seat, behind the wheel and closed his door. There was a woman in the front seat, too. It was eerily quiet inside, as if they had shut out not just the wind, but the sound of it, too.

"My name's Don." He offered his hand across the seatback and Victor shook it. "Mine's Victor," he said.

"This is my wife, Ellie, and that's our boy, Robbie." The wife nodded and smiled wanly at him. The boy only continued to stare at him from his dark corner.

"Where were you headed?" Victor asked, more to make conversation than because he really cared.

"Pennsylvania," Don said. "My wife's mom, she's got a farm there, told us we could live with her a bit if we could make it there. We started out yesterday, figured we had enough for the gas, but then a tire went, and we had no spare, so we had to replace that, and there went the last of our gas money. It's a good sixty miles or more yet. I could probably make it, walking, but Ellie, she's expecting, she'd never make it, nor the boy, and I can't just leave them here."

Victor saw the boy's crutch, then, shoved into the corner behind him, and he looked down at the one shriveled leg. No, of course, you couldn't walk sixty miles on a crutch, with one bad leg.

The boy—Robbie, was that it?—saw him glance at the crutch and gave him back a scornful look. "Daddy, I'm hungry," he said.

"I know, son, I know," Don said. "We'll just have to wait until...well, we'll just have to wait, is all."

"I've got some food," Victor said impulsively. He regretted the words as soon as they were out of his mouth, but it was too late to take them back. Husband and wife looked over the seat at him, but Robbie stared meaningfully at the white paper bag under Victor's arm.

"It's just some old rolls and stuff," Victor said. He shoved the bag at the boy, feeling resentful, and somehow outmaneuvered, although he didn't exactly understand how, or by whom. "Here. Take it."

Robbie snatched the bag from his hand and tore it open. "There's all kinds of rolls and things, Ma," he said. He started to take one, and looked at his mother. "It's okay, ain't it? He said we could."

"You sure?" she asked, looking directly at Victor. He wanted to change his mind, say, no, I think I will keep them for myself after all, but her voice and her look were so plaintive, that he nodded his head and said, ""It's okay. Someone gave them to me, so I guess I'm just passing them on."

The boy took a big cinnamon roll, and handed the sack to his mother, and she took some kind of scone, and passed the bag on to her husband. He wolfed down a Danish and the bag went round again.

"You don't want none?" Don asked, crumbs stuck to his lips.

Victor swallowed. "No, I ate just a little bit ago, I'm stuffed, thank you. You folks go ahead."

They did, eating in silence, chewing frantically. He wondered how long it had been since they ate. The bag was empty in a minute or so. He watched regretfully as Don crumpled it up and dropped it on the floor by his feet.

"Well, I reckon we won't starve, at least," Don said. "We are surely grateful to you for sharing."

"Yes, we thank you mightily," Ellie said, and fixed her eyes on her son. "Robbie?"

"Thank you," he mumbled with no sign of sincerity, licking the last ghost of flavor off his fingers.

"This place you're going, in Pennsylvania," Victor said, "How much gas do you think it would take to get there?"

"Not too much. This old bus, she eats gas, but even so, I expect ten dollars worth would see us there," Don said. He sighed, and looked at the frosted over windshield. "Might as well be ten thousand, though, I guess. There's nobody out tonight. You're the first person to come by in an hour or more."

They sat in silence for a long time. Victor thought of the money in his pocket, and those motels across town. Even if he could get to them, there was no guarantee that anyone would rent him a room for the money he had, and once he got there, he would be that much further away from anywhere else. If he went the other direction, he could probably make it to the Seven Eleven. He could get hot coffee there, and a hot dog, and probably they would let him hang out for a while, maybe the rest of the night, if he caused no trouble.

He took the crumpled bills out of his pocket. "I've got," he said, and paused to count them, as if he didn't know exactly how many there were. "I've got eleven dollars here. I could let you have seven of them, if you think that will be enough."

Don's eyes widened hopefully. "I expect it might. Anyway, if we got within a couple of miles, we might be able to hoof it the rest of the way, or maybe I could get there and bring somebody back for them. Her mother's got an old pickup, or she might even have a can of gas. For sure we could get close enough. Only...." He took his eyes off the money and looked at Victor. "Only, it don't seem right, taking your money. I mean, we already ate your food, and seeing as that's all you got."

"Oh, that doesn't matter, I've got someplace I was headed, I just have to get there. Here." He handed Don seven dollars, and then added another one to them. That left him three. That would get him a coffee and a hot dog, or a donut, anyway.

"Well, if you're sure?" Don gave his wife a look. She licked her lips and held her breath. "I've got a gas can in the back, I'll walk to that Sheetz station we passed a bit ago, and get enough gas to drive us there. You want to wait here, in the car? Say, you could come to Pennsylvania with us, if you like."

"No, I got some place I got to go," Victor said. He flung open the car door and got out quick, before the wind could come in after him. Before, he thought grimly, they could wish him a Merry Christmas, but he was too late. Don said it, and then Ellie, and even little Robbie.

"Same to you," he said back, closing the door, and started off. He cursed himself for a fool all over again. Here he was now, in nothing but a light windbreaker, his food all gone, and nothing but three dollars in his pocket. Talk about your Merry Christmases.

* * * * * * *

He wasn't sure how far he had walked, or how long—he was light headed now, and he could scarcely feel his feet, lifting and coming down in the snow—when the little girl walked up to him, seeming to come out of nowhere. She was dressed in white, and her face was so pale, she could almost have been conjured up by the snow.

"Mister," she said without preamble. "I am so cold and hungry, and I got no place to go."

"Oh, hell's bells," he said aloud. He ought to have known, he thought angrily, the way this damned night was going. He yanked the last three dollars out of his pocket and thrust it toward her, but to his surprise, she took a step back from him and did not take it.

"It won't work if you resent giving it," she said. "You have to let it go."

"Won't work? Won't work for what?" There was a buzzing in his head, like a host of wasps was in there. He handed the money to her again, but she only shook her head.

He dropped to his knees in the snow and took hold of her shoulders. She felt thin as a bird.

"You are one strange little girl," he said. "I been giving and giving all night, and you're the first one refused to take."

"You have to share it. Not what we give, but what we share, for the gift without the giver is bare."

He smiled into her face despite everything. There was something about her, a luminescence. She almost seemed to glow in the dark and the falling snow.

"I don't understand what you are saying," he said. He had a vague idea there was something else, earlier this evening, that he hadn't understood either, but he was too tired and cold to think straight.

"If you bless it, we will both share in the blessing."

"Well, then, if that's the way of it," he said wearily. "Take it then, and I surely do bless it, and I bless you."

She did take the money then from his frozen fingers. Hers felt oddly warm when he touched them. She closed her eyes and looked down, and seemed to be praying. He closed his too, and tried what she said, tried to let the money go, to bless it.

He thought, out of the blue, of his mother again, of an incident when he had been just a boy, he couldn't have been more than eight or nine. His mother had loaded up a basket of food from their cellar, to take to an aunt who was doing poorly. Mostly, in the winter, they lived on what she had put up in the cellar, and seeing the jars disappear from the shelves, he had said, "Won't we need this food before the winter is out?"

She had given him a stern look, and said, "I never have been and never will be too poor to share what I have, because that is the worst kind of poverty: that is the poverty of the spirit."

Yes, she was right, and the little girl, too. He had given what he had, but he hadn't let go of it, he hadn't shared it. He had resented everything that he had given, and his resentment had held on to everything even when it was gone from his possession. He thought back on his coat, and made an effort to bless the warmth that it might give the old man, and he thought of the family huddled in their car, and blessed the food he had given them, and the money; and the little girl...he opened his eyes, but she was gone.

Probably she was somewhere looking for shelter, or more likely, something to eat. He hoped she found it, before the night got any worse. The snow seemed to be coming down harder now, although, oddly, he didn't feel anywhere near as cold as he had before. He felt hot, if anything. He undid a couple of buttons, and stumbled to his feet. He was light headed, though. He couldn't exactly think where he was, or where he was headed. No place, really, he supposed. He had no place to go, did he, and nothing to do when he got there?

He began to stagger through the snow, singing softly to himself. "What child is this...?"

"Mister?"

He looked, and there was the girl again, right beside him. "Why, I thought you had gone," he said. "Why'd you want to hang around, anyway? You ought to be looking for something to eat. The Seven Eleven is open, I bet, if I knew which way that was."

"Come with me," she said, and took hold of his hand.

He held back, but she tugged at him. "Hurry," she said. "This way."

"Well, that's just a back alley," he said, "There isn't going to be anything down that way."

But there was. They came round the corner, and the night fled before the light that spilled out of the windows ahead of them, and the lamp shining over the door, and the sign that said, Antoinette's.

He stopped in his tracks, gaping in astonishment, and while he stared, the door of the restaurant opened, and there Antoinette herself framed in it, she looked a lot like Karen Delvecchio. She saw him and smiled, and waved.

"Hurry, come on in," she called to him.

"Little girl," he started to say, but she had disappeared again, and when he looked down, he saw only his own footprints in the snow.

Why, there she was, in the doorway with Antoinette, and as he stared, the others came out and crowded around them, too—the old man, still in the blue parka, and the family from the car, Don and Ellie, he could see now that she was pregnant, and Robbie, balanced on his crutch.

"Come on," they called to him, and "Supper's ready," and "The fire is warm."

"We're all just waiting for you," Ellie said, "Hurry, now."

He did. He began to run, and then he was flying, and they waved and called, and Antoinette laughed gaily and said, "Welcome, come on in, welcome to Antoinette's."

THE MUSHROOM KING

It is a paradox of sorts that though they are often people who most enjoy solitude, writers are nonetheless inevitably intrigued by people. This is not to say that they do not dislike some of them or find themselves bored with them. Still, I have said often that even boring people fascinate me.

Mr. Maugham said that he never spent fifteen minutes in the company of another person that he couldn't have written a story about. I have no doubt that he was speaking sincerely. I can certainly say that I have never spent fifteen minutes in the company of another person that I didn't discover something of interest about him or her (well, yes, all right, there have been times when the fifteen minutes seemed like fifteen years).

I have always found people infinitely fascinating. This is something that I have discovered about my fellow men and women over the years: everyone—but everyone—has something special about them, something they do better than anyone else, something they know better than anyone else, some secret that you may be the first to ferret out of them, some unsuspected (perhaps even by themselves) talent or gift. Every one has his niche.

Let me tell you, for instance, about Otis McVeigh, as I shall call him. I went to school back in Ohio with Otis. Otis was quite simply a clunk. He was not the stupidest person I have ever met, though he never displayed any great intelligence. That is not the same as saying he had none—for some bizarre reason, straight young men in the Midwest of the fifties had an aversion to letting it be known they had brains. I had yet another classmate who, if memory serves, was never more than a C student, who later turned out to be a professor at the University of California in Los Angeles, a job you don't get without some smarts.

What was worse in Otis' case was that he had no wit. He was neither good-looking nor spectacularly unattractive. He was not unkind nor rude nor evil, which can at least be fascinating. If, some years back, you should have asked me if there weren't at least one exception to finding something interesting in everyone I met, I might have been tempted to mention Otis.

Some years after our school days had ended, I was back in Ohio to visit my mother. It was spring. Mushroom season. Which is to say, sponge mushrooms—morels if you want to be fancy—but to us they were sponge mushrooms. Oh, to be sure there were some sub-categories. Dog's peckers looked like, well, you know, and were among the least prized. But mostly we called them sponge mushrooms, and they did indeed look like little brown and golden sponges on their all too fragile stems.

In Ohio mushroom season is brief, two or perhaps three weeks. The weather must be just right. A good shower and the following day a warm sun. They often come back to the same field where they were found the year before, but some springs they hardly make an appearance, and even when they lie at your feet in abundance they are so well camouflaged that they can be all but impossible to see. It is not uncommon for a hunter to return home with his sack no fuller than when he set out. Locals tend to guard their favorite spots with a secrecy that would be envied by a James Bond villain.

On this occasion, on the first morning of my visit, my mother fixed me an omelet filled with the precious delicacies and the butter they had soaked up—enormous, meaty, savory specimens. Between mouthfuls I asked her where she had found such bounty. She smiled a bit shame-facedly and told me she had paid a visit to Otis.

"Otis?" I almost choked on my food. "Not Otis McVeigh?"

The very same, as it turned out. "He's the Mushroom King,"

my mother explained.

It seems that though others might spend hours in the woods and return home empty-handed, Otis had no such problem. He found mushrooms by the sack full, by the basket. He was never, during the season, without a generous supply of them, which he was more than happy to sell to those less fortunate.

Of course everyone wanted to know where he found them. Mushroom hunting is serious business in Ohio, in the springtime. Each morning during the season there were those who would attempt to follow Otis when he left his house, to discover where his particular fields of plenty might be; but to no avail. Around and around Otis would drive, down country roads and rutted lanes, through covered bridges, past this barn and over this hillock, into town once more and out another route—until he had lost his trackers or they had given up in disgust.

Later (unless their own search had been fruitful, and supposing they really craved some fruits of the field, as by this time they surely did) they must park at the curb outside Otis' house, follow the cement walk along the side of the house to the back porch, knock at his kitchen door and purchase—at a hefty price—the objects of their desire. I am even told that there were those who came late at night, under cover of darkness, and afterward pretended that they had found these mushrooms themselves. But I am quite certain that my mother would never have stooped to such subterfuge.

There was nothing for it. I had to see for myself. My mother placed a call and that very evening we found ourselves following the cement walk about the side of Otis' house, only a short stroll from my mother's own.

Otis gave every sign of being happy to see me, though we had never been chums in any sense of the word. He invited us into his kitchen. We sat at a big round table covered with oilcloth. There was a murmur of voices from a television, or perhaps a radio, in another part of the house. The aroma of cooked cabbage and the dishes stacked neatly in the sink spoke of an early supper. Otis and I struggled to make conversation, as people will who wish to be polite but have little to say to one another. Finally I mentioned that we had hoped to buy some mushrooms.

He went to his pantry and returned with what he said were his very best, just picked that same day. They were in a shoebox lined with a clean, neatly folded dishtowel, a dozen or more of the loveliest mushrooms I had ever seen. The largest of them was a giant, easily seven inches tall, and there were a good half dozen who were only a shade smaller.

I looked them over, holding them one at a time in my hand. They were all but weightless, clean, smelling faintly of the earth from which they had recently come—the scent of dead leaves and cleansing rains and an unspoiled wood in the springtime sun. It is a scent like no other and the finest of perfumes to the aficionado.

We bought six of them, which Otis put into a brown paper bag for us. As I was counting out the money, I glanced up once and found him looking at me with an expression that I could not read and which vanished so quickly I thought perhaps I had imagined it. Was that a twinkle in his eyes, a spark of amusement? I blinked and looked again, and now I saw nothing but the dull gaze with which in the past he had always regarded the world.

We shook hands and parted with the usual polite suggestions to look one another up again. But I was disconcerted. That sense of having surprised something heretofore unsuspected in his expression teased at my mind. Had I missed something all along about Otis? I have always counted myself an astute judge of other people—that, after all, is the essence of the writer's business. It was troubling to think that I might have been entirely off the mark where Otis was concerned.

As we strolled homeward, I asked my mother what she thought of Otis, what impression she got of him. She thought for a moment and said, "He seems very contented."

As she so often did, my mother had hit the nail precisely on the head. Real contentment is far rarer than one might suppose. In most people you can almost always sense a feeling of wanting, of needing, of searching for something more than, different from, their present circumstances. Sometimes it is only a wish for the workday to end, or dinnertime to arrive, the trivia of a day's impatience, and sometimes it is great ambition, and sometimes great resentment at ambition thwarted.

There are few who you feel are truly satisfied in any given moment with their lot. Walking at my mother's side on that moonlit Ohio night, with Otis' mushrooms in a bag in my hand and the memory of that glint of amusement I had seen earlier still fresh in my mind, I realized that Otis was one of those rare few.

I had to laugh, partly at myself. Who would ever have dreamed that there would be a story to tell about poor Otis, but there it was. He had found his niche.

He was the Mushroom King.

(Excerpted from *Spine Intact, Some Creases*)

I'LL SEE YOU HOME

It had been a bad year: a slow spring, the crops late planted, and just when they had been about to harvest, winter came ahead of himself, so they lost more of the wheat than they reaped, and most of the corn. They would have to make the long trip into town to buy provisions, if they weren't to starve over the winter, but money was short, and she had put off going just one day too long. When Janet finally said they must go, as the larder was nearly empty, another storm came out of nowhere, and she stood at the stove, stirring the oatmeal—all they had left now— the baby balanced at her hip, and watched the white outside the window, and worried.

It snowed for two days, and when finally there was a pause in its falling, Tom went outside and looked at the few sullen stars in the distant sky, and said they would go in the morning, and pray to get back before the weather changed its mind.

So they hitched Big Gray to the wagon in the first chilly light of dawn. She would have to go with him. He would need help loading and unloading the wagon if they were to have it done before dark, and the boys were needed here to see to the chores. They couldn't do them, though, and keep an eye on the baby, and anyway, Rachel was only six months and still feeding, and so she must come with them to town, cold or no.

The roads were treacherous still with snow, and Big Gray was old, but as enormous as his name implied, a giant of a horse, and though his strength was clearly on the wane, he was strong enough still to pull the wagon through ruts and drifts with no great effort. Janet sat beside Tom, the baby Rachel bundled on her lap. If everything went well, they would get there and load their provisions and make it home before dark.

Things weren't going well, though, they hadn't since that late spring, and even in the wan daylight, the road was not a good one. Halfway into town, Tom missed a bad rut, and they broke a wheel. There was nothing for it but that he must repair it, and that took a considerable while, so that, by the time they reached town, and bought what they needed, and loaded it into the wagon, and started for home, the day was already quit, night falling, and with it, fresh snow.

The night got quickly darker, and the snow fell harder, whipped now by a merciless wind, and Big Gray, plodding through ever-deeper drifts, began to tire, you could see the slump in his shoulders, and the way his hooves sometimes lost their rhythm.

Rachel began to cry, and Janet opened her coat and her dress and nursed her, shielding her from the cold as best she could with the blanket. Even so, her breast felt icy, and she cut the feeding short. Rachel protested and then, once again wrapped in the warmth of the blanket, slept.

"We'll have to take the short cut," Tom said. It was the first he had spoken since they left town, and she knew that his silence was a worried one.

"In the dark?" she said, alarmed. "We'll never get across the bridge."

"We'll never make it home the long way," he said. "Don't you trouble yourself over that bridge, I'll get you both home safely, you have my promise on that."

So he took the cut through the woods, and down the long hill, to the ravine over the creek, and the bridge that spanned it, no more than logs and planks, with a scant inch or two to spare on either side, and Gray didn't like the crossing at the best of times, in summer, and in daylight. He balked, as they had known he would.

Tom got down from the wagon, and took the reins, and

gentled the horse onto the planks. They were slippery, and the wagon slid sideways a little, and Janet caught her breath. It was twenty feet or more down to the creek, and that was nothing now but ice and rocks—but the wheels held.

They went slowly, Tom talking to Big Gray the whole way, his words no more than a murmur to Janet's ears, and she began to think they would be all right, when something spooked the horse. Maybe a hoof slipped. She never did know what, but he jerked and reared back, and Tom swore aloud, and the wagon slid again. This time, the back right wheel went over the edge.

On the slick bridge, the old horse's footing was precarious, and the drag of the wagon's weight pulling him back and sideways threw him off-balance, and just like that, they went down, man and horse, went down hard.

Janet sat there in frozen silence for a long moment, clutching little Rachel to her bosom, and waiting to see if the wagon was going over, but it stayed where it was.

"Tom?" she said finally, in a small voice.

It seemed to take him a long time to answer, but finally he said, "It's all right, love, I'll get you down from there," and a moment after that he loomed beside her in the darkness.

"But what will we do?" she asked, clambering down with his help.

"Gray's broken a leg," he said. "We'll have to leave him, and walk home."

"From here? But it's three miles, most of. In this weather? We'll freeze to death before we get there."

"There's nothing else for it now," he said, and added, in a determined voice, "Never you fear, my love, I swore I'd see you both home and I will, and safely, and the boys can come back tomorrow with the sleds and bring things up to the house."

Old Gray cried in his pain, and rolled his frightened eyes at her. She cast a tearful glance in his direction, but there was nothing they could do for him, and she set out with her husband, and her baby in her arms.

They had not gone far before he stopped and took off his long heavy coat, heavier than hers because he spent more time out of doors than she did, and put it about her shoulders.

"Tom, you'll freeze to death," she said.

"Oh, it will take more than this little bit of a chill to do me in," he said, and would not take the coat back

It was hard going. The wind beat at them and spat snow in their faces. The cold was bitter, and she thought surely there had never been a night so black outside of hell. The snow had drifted waist high in places, so that they could not step out of it but must push their way through, and Janet was tired in no time. She stumbled, and would have fallen more than once were it not for his strong arm about her shoulders. Even through the coats, hers and his, the cold was bitter, and she could not imagine what he must be suffering.

"Just lift one foot, and put it down," Tom said, "That's how the journey's done, my darling."

Which she did. The hill up from the ravine was long and, in places, steep, and that took the breath out of you. It was little easier walking when the ground leveled off, but here the trees were thinner, and the wind got at you more fiercely.

"Almost home," Tom said, and then, finally, they came out of the trees, and there was the clearing, and in the distance, the light of the cabin.

Here, though, she did fall, buried over her head in the smothering snow, and she thought she could go no further, and said, "I'm done for, Tom, take the baby and go."

He would not hear of it. "I said I'd see you safely home," he said. He got her somehow to her feet, and said, "We'll run now, it'll get the blood moving," and run they did, staggering, reeling, her chest afire and her feet beyond feeling, and they got to the steps up to the door, and she fell again, and this time, she hadn't the strength to rise.

The boys had been waiting anxiously for them, though, and they heard her and ran to the door, and Bill, the oldest, took the baby and rushed her to her crib, and Abe got Janet to the rocker in front of the fire.

She had no sooner dropped into the chair, though, than she cried aloud, "Oh, you wicked boys, you've left your father to freeze on the steps."

The boys looked puzzled at one another, and went to the door and opened it. "There's no one here, Ma," Bill said after a moment.

She got up and came herself to look, standing in the mocking wind. There, where the snow was crushed down, was where she had lain on the steps a moment before, and in the distance, just before the trees, the dark stain where she had fallen and Tom had had to lift her up, and between there and here, the staggering footsteps—but only the one set of them. Just hers.

"We'll go and look for him," Bill said, and they went to fetch their coats, but she sat down heavily in the chair again, and studied the shivering flames, and said, "No, let it be. Morning will do."

The boys did not argue. They brought her hot broth, and when she had drunk it, she nursed little Rachel, letting her have her fill this time. The cabin trembled in the wind, and whimpered, and little tufts of snow wept on the sills.

* * * * * * *

The storm was over by morning, a petulant sun glowering down on the devastation that had been done.

The boys bundled themselves up and took the sleds, and followed the trail she had left, her footsteps mostly filled in by now, but enough of them still to show the way, and once they had entered the trees, the trail was clearer.

They traveled the woods, and down the long hill to the ravine, and they found him there, his head bent grotesquely, his neck broken where Gray had fallen upon him, man and horse both frozen solid.

"What I don't understand," Abe would say whenever they told the story, and Bill would always click his tongue and shake his head, "What I don't understand, is how he got his coat out from under, and put it about her, as she would surely have frozen without it, that night was so cold."

ANNE'S WEDDING NIGHT

AUTHOR'S NOTE: This is France between the revolutions. Anne has been jilted by her lover and, to save her family from financial ruin, married to the wealthy Baron de Brussac, whom she despises. It is her wedding night.

It was not likely that Anne would remain morose for very long.

She was young and high-spirited, used to laughing a great deal and enjoying life. Moreover, it was a warm summer night and a ball was in progress; this was the native land, in a manner of speaking, of her soul, and she trod it with the expertise of one born to the realm.

She danced with her papa and after him with a gentleman as old as him who regarded her with the frankest lust in his eyes.

And she danced with the soldier who had kissed her hand.

His name was Guy, and he came from Provence. When he smiled, he smiled with the languor and indolence of the hot southern coast, as Italian as it was French. He told her she was as beautiful as the banks of flowers that bloomed above the sea there. She laughed delightedly and sipped the champagne he brought her when the dance was ended.

Already she was enjoying the party more; after all, what had changed? She was married, that was all. And she was rich. She did not have much grasp of money matters and so had only the vaguest idea of how rich she was, but she was sure her new husband's wealth was vast.

If she wanted, she could have balls such as this every week— even every day. Of course, they would not be wedding balls, but this was Paris; one needed no excuse to throw a party.

With her husband's wealth and her own beauty and charm, she would become the most famous hostess in Paris. Perhaps she would have a salon, like Mademoiselle Rivière. People— men—would vie with one another for invitations, and she would lead them in glittering conversation; She did not know exactly what was talked about at such salons, but she had never been at a loss for words. She would have the most famous, the most interesting people—and, of course, the handsomest men.

She suddenly imagined Émile standing at the door of her home (they would need something grander than this townhouse, something more suited to the entertainments she had in mind), pleading for entrance. At last she would let him come in. He would be without Louise, of course. Should she let him dance with her or not? Perhaps she would let him suffer while she flirted with all the handsome men flocking around her, courting her, courting her favor.

Her husband was conspicuously absent from these fancies.

She sipped more champagne. She danced with the minister of fine arts. She danced with a young man who said he had been to America.

And she danced with the young soldier again.

The third time she danced with him, he held her very close and whispered in her ear, "Aren't you warm from all this dancing?"

"A little."

"Let's go outside for a breath of air."

"I...."

"No one will notice. Look, here we are."

She saw that while they danced he had steered her deftly to the doors that opened onto the terrace at the side of the house, away from the gawking crowd in front. Now, taking her hesitation for assent, he led her out onto the darkened terrace.

She would have objected, but the fresh air did feel so good.

She had not realized how warm and flushed she was from the champagne, the dancing. She felt giddy and breathless. Was this what it felt like to be tipsy?

"Why are you so sad?" he asked.

"Does it show?"

"Yes—to me, at least."

She did not answer. She had stopped in the rectangle of light that fell through the open door, but he led her toward the deeper shadows under the chestnut tree.

"I was thinking of running away," she said. Actually she had not thought of it at all until the words had seemed to slip from her lips, but now she considered the possibility. What would they say if she just kept on her way, out the postern gate, through the darkened streets to—to where?

"Perhaps your marriage will not be so bad," he said.

"Perhaps, perhaps. I'm sick of perhaps," she said. "If only one could know...." She was talking nonsense and knew it. She couldn't think why her head was so muddled.

"That's always the question, isn't it—whether to trade a known present, however unpleasant, for an unknown future."

But for her it was too late, the trade had already been made. The future was unknown and the past was lost to her.

"Anne," he murmured. They had reached the deep shadows under the tree, and he turned her toward him. She had a sense of *déjà-vu*, of having been here before. The warm, scented darkness; the handsome young man. He stood half in shadow, half in moonlight, so that she could see the shiny buttons of his uniform but not his face. He was so tall, so broad-shouldered... she hadn't meant to kiss him.

"Émile...."

If he noticed that she called him by another's name, or cared, he gave no sign. He gathered her into his arms, his lips fastening hungrily upon her trembling ones.

But he wasn't Émile, and this wasn't the same; this was foolish at best. She put her hands flat against his chest, meaning to end the kiss, to insist that they return to the ball inside. In a flash of insight rare for her, she saw how badly she was behaving and was ashamed of her actions.

She felt the young soldier suddenly stiffen. He took a step back from her, so abruptly that she swayed off balance and had to put her hand on his arm.

"Please," she said, before she realized that he was not looking at her at all, but beyond her. His face was pale, the laughter gone from his eyes.

"Yes, please indeed, Monsieur."

It was her husband's voice, icy cold. She turned to find he had followed them onto the terrace. He regarded them both with a look of barely contained fury.

"Monsieur le Baron...." The guardsman attempted to speak but Jean ignored him and, turning his back, went to the door opening onto the ball. Anne felt a strange surprise to see that it was still going on exactly as it had been.

"Philippe!" Jean barked his majordomo's name. Several of the guests looked curiously in his direction, but he ignored them.

"Philippe!"

The majordomo appeared, hurrying through the crowd.

"Have the carriage brought around at once," Jean ordered.

The servant looked confused.

"At once," Jean repeated. He turned back to his wife and the soldier.

"As for you," he addressed Guy, "you will leave my house immediately, before I have you whipped like a dog and thrown into the streets."

The guardsman was twenty years young and nearly a head taller; ordinarily the young man would have challenged such a remark, but something about the look in the other man's eyes and the tone of his voice gave him pause.

He clicked his heels smartly and bowed. "Monsieur, my apologies," he said. He strode briskly away, disappearing inside without so much as a backward glance at Anne. She might have been, she thought, some *fille de joie* that he had picked up off the streets.

She was left alone in the moonlight with her enraged husband. Shock and fear had cleared her head of any befuddlement, and she stared wide-eyed back at him as he turned his attention to her.

"My dear," he said, speaking with frigid contempt, "did you really think I would allow you to give to someone else what I paid so dearly for?"

She managed the courage to say, "How dare you!" but he was not interested in her remarks or her indignation. He seized her wrist in a grip so harsh it sent a jolt of pain up her arm.

"Come with me," he said.

"Let go of me, I won't."

But she did, because she had no choice. He fairly dragged her back into the ball and through it, past the startled faces of their wedding guests. He looked neither right nor left, nor did he so much as pause, even when her mother came running up white-faced.

"What's wrong?" Mama cried, but they rushed right on by her.

"Where are you taking me?" Anne demanded; he made no answer.

A lackey rushed to open the front door, and for a moment Anne thought he meant to have her whipped and thrown into the street as he had threatened to do with the soldier.

The carriage came clattering into the courtyard, the driver hastily trying to button his coat as he came. It stopped, and before the footman could hurry down to open the door, Jean had dragged her to it and, throwing the door open, shoved her forcibly inside.

He's mad, she thought, terrified. She looked desperately at the crowd that had followed them to the door, but although they all watched in astonishment, no one moved to intervene. This was her husband, after all, dragging her about like a piece of baggage. Husbands did what they would with their wives; it was the order of things. And it sometimes made for delicious gossip.

Jean spoke to the driver—she was in too much of a state

to even try to hear what he said—and then he, too, climbed into the carriage, slamming the door, and a moment later it lumbered off, clattering across the stones of the courtyard. The gates were opened; the crowd outside parted before them. The wedding guests gaped after them, some of them bewildered, others plainly amused. *Tiens,* they would not soon forget this wedding ball.

For Anne, it was too much to bear—the humiliation, being dragged away in the middle of the ball and carried off to God alone knew where, still dressed in her wedding gown. She began to cry, sobbing noisily into her hands. Once he moved on the seat beside her, and she threw herself into the far corner of the carriage.

"Don't touch me," she cried, but apparently he had no interest in touching her; he was only making himself more comfortable.

She became increasingly angry as they went along. She was cool without a wrap of any kind. She had no idea how long they would be out because she had no idea where they were going and disdained to ask. They drove through the darkened streets of Paris, only occasionally passing another carriage or some foot traffic. She could hear shouts in the distance from time to time. Once she thought she saw a pale glow in the sky and wondered if it could already be dawn, but she dismissed the idea at once; she knew it could be no more than midnight.

The coach came to a halt. Glancing out, she saw some soldiers on horseback talking to the driver. Her husband got out of the carriage and went forward to talk to them himself. She leaned as far out the window as she dared, trying to get the gist of their conversation.

"...Another uprising," she heard, and, "They've barricaded the streets...burning...fighting going on...."

One word, snatched from all the others, made her shudder and draw fearfully back into the carriage; she heard one of the soldiers say, "Revolution."

Another revolution! It struck terror into her aristocratic heart. It had been forty years since the Great Revolution, but no one of her class had ever forgotten what happened. She had not been born then, of course, but she knew the stories. Her own grandfather on her mother's side had taken that horrible ride to the guillotine, and one of her aunts had been slain by the mobs. Surely not even her madman of a husband would risk remaining out on a night such as this one.

The soldiers rode away. Looking out, she saw her husband talking earnestly to the driver. She heard him say, "We'll take the rue Bercy," as he turned and strode back to the carriage.

"Are we going home?" she asked when the carriage started up again. They were the first words she had spoken to him since ordering him not to touch her.

He did not answer, but when he turned to look at her, she cringed inwardly. The answer was written plain on his face. He hated her. He would not care if they were killed by the Parisian mobs.

"In the name of God," she cried, "if you will not think of me, think of yourself, what good—"

She stopped short in mid-sentence. The carriage had been speeding along, but now as they rounded a corner it halted again. They had only to glance from the window to see why.

The street ahead was barricaded with wood, furniture, even an overturned buggy. Standing on either side of the barricade were peasants, armed with guns, pitchforks, axes, even rocks. A block or so beyond them a house was afire, its flames providing an eerie light that silhouetted the peasants and sent their shadows dancing crazily along the street.

Shouts went up as the men at the barricade saw the carriage. She heard someone shout, "You there, driver, bring the coach up here where we can have a look."

Her husband leaned out the window and called to the driver, "Turn around."

The carriage began to turn, the driver reining the horses forward, back, forward again, trying to work the vehicle around in the narrow space. The horses whinnied nervously, scenting the danger.

The men at the barricade shouted again when they saw what was happening, and several began to run toward the carriage. Anne's window was turned toward them now and she watched in fascinated terror as they came closer, closer—she could see the sweat gleaming on their faces and she fancied she saw the maniacal light in their eyes.

One of the men raised a gun. "Stop, or we'll shoot," he yelled.

The carriage was around. The driver cracked the whip and the horses leapt forward, sending the carriage rocking and swaying wildly.

"Get back, you fool," her husband said, yanking her roughly out of the way of the window.

A gun fired. Something struck the rear of the coach. Anne sat huddled in terror as they clattered pell-mell through the now-haunted streets. The coach tilted crazily back and forth, knocking her first this way and then that.

What if they overturned? What if those men caught them? She had horrible visions of herself dragged screaming through the streets, led to a waiting guillotine. She began to cry again.

"Oh, Mama, where is Mama?" she sobbed hysterically.

The carriage skittered around yet another corner, and again came to an abrupt stop. Two men blocked the way, one with a pitchfork in his hands, the other with a musket. The street was little more than an alley, too narrow for them to go around the men or to attempt to turn again.

They were trapped!

Anne whimpered helplessly into her hands, unable to prevent herself from watching wide-eyed as the two men approached. The one with the pitchfork remained in the center of the road in front of the horses, blocking the way. The other, with the musket, came to the carriage. He said something to the driver, then, barely pausing, came back to where they sat. His face suddenly appeared in the window. She saw that he was looking directly at her, his eyes feverish with excitement, his lips curved in an ugly snarl of a smile. He laughed, and it made her want to scream with terror.

She did not see the pistol appear in her husband's hands, nor where it came from. He suddenly lifted it to the window and fired point-blank into the grinning face.

The face seemed to explode from within. Drops of blood and pieces of something else she did not want to name spattered inside the carriage, staining the leather upholstery and the white skirt of her wedding gown.

She slumped back into the corner with a sigh and fainted dead away.

(Excerpted from *This Splendid Earth*)

NEW KID IN TOWN

She had never regretted marrying him. He was the loveliest man, and certainly she had nothing to complain about. If any man knew how to treat a woman like a queen...nothing too good for her, nothing she could ask for that wasn't forthcoming at once; and there was little to ask for, as far as that went, little he hadn't already thought of himself and seen to. How could a woman complain about a man like that?

He was good company, too. He was certainly the most intelligent man she had ever known, and better still, he had never lost that sense of humor that had attracted her to him in the first place. Contrary to what most men believed, it really was not the handsomest man that caught a woman's fancy. A woman likes a man who makes her laugh. She had always thought that old rogue Don Juan was probably a better wit than he was a lover.

And Arthur was successful. Everyone knew him, or knew of him, at any rate. And everyone looked up to him. Women eyed him favorably and men respected him. If you judged a man by how others saw him, you would have to say he was unquestionably the lord of his domain.

"Long day today," he said, stripping off his clothes. "Getting those fellows to agree on anything—a dozen of them, a dozen different opinions."

"You should lay down the law," she said. "You are the one who decides things, after all."

"Oh, I like them to feel they're a part of everything, you know what I mean? I want them to feel that we're all equals."

He leaned down to kiss her cheek fondly, and put out the light, and got onto his side of the bed. She waited, not moving herself, not wanting to seem demanding, or needy; but he did not turn toward her.

She suppressed a sigh. Well, there was that. It was no good denying it: he was old. Of course, that was not why she had married him, but still, she was young, young enough to miss what was increasingly lacking in their marriage.

She thought he was already drifting off to sleep, but he surprised her by asking, "What did you think of the new man?"

She hesitated. Had he seen the looks that passed between them? But what were looks, anyway, where was the sin of looking? Still, she picked her words carefully.

"He seems earnest," she said.

"Earnest?" He laughed softly. "Yes, he's that all right. A real hell-brand, looks like to me. I expect I'll have my hands full with that young man, keeping him on a leash."

After a moment, she asked, in the most careful tone she could muster, "What did you say his name was?"

"Lancelot," he said.

Lancelot. She smiled into the darkness and turned the name over and about in her mind. It had a musical lilt to it, didn't it? *Lancelot.*

IN A SMALL TOWN

Eaton, Ohio, where I grew up, is an old town. It was begun in 1792 in an Ohio that was then the Wild West. It started with a fort, Fort Saint Clair.

The Fort has long since burned away but there is still the very pretty Fort Saint Clair Park just at the edge of town, with its wide green lawns (scene of annual civil war reenactments) and its all but unspoiled woods and meandering stream. There is the Whispering Oak as well, in which Chief Little Turtle of the Miami Tribe hid (according to legend, though history is less sure) to listen to the soldiers make their plans and so was able to massacre them later—which makes him, I suppose, the true forerunner of today's gossip mavens who make a business of massacring people with collected whispers.

The town which soon grew up in the vicinity is lovely, too. Like all towns and cities these days it has suffered some from the relentless march of progress. A tornado some forty years ago destroyed the lovely old Victoria Opera House, which was then in use as the City Building. It was replaced with a hideous cement block architecture.

Though it was spared by the tornado, the splendid old Victorian library building—admittedly a monstrosity but a monstrosity of infinite fascination—was deemed too decrepit to be maintained and repaired (a fate I fear I shall face before too many years have passed by) and was torn down. In its stead is a perfectly harmless, and charmless, modern structure. I understand the benefits of its modernity but books seem to me to fit better in a Victorian structure, in much the same way that banking belongs to chunky, granite, Georgian styled buildings. I can never quite feel that my money is safe in a building made largely of glass.

Still, the wide, tree-lined streets remain and many Victorian houses and the Greek revival courthouse that occupies much of the central block downtown. Though the Seven Mile Tavern, which once graced its banks, was lost years ago to a fire, the Seven Mile Creek still follows its circuitous and beautiful path through the town. Where it widens below the Main Street Bridge the creek forms Crystal Lake, which is really not much more than a pond but a very pretty site nonetheless. In winter it freezes over and ice skaters add to its charm.

There is a covered bridge over the creek too, the Roberts bridge, the second oldest covered bridge in the United States and oldest of the nation's six remaining double-barreled or shotgun bridges, which is to say it has two passages side by side.

When I was young there were a great number of these covered bridges on the roads around Eaton but most have gone, many of them burned. Farmers, the rumors say, who could not drive their enormous equipment through the narrow bridges and so were forced to go many miles around to get just across the creek. I cannot say for sure, but it would not surprise me if the rumors were true. Farmers are used to taking things down and starting them up again. But covered bridges, of course, do not grow on trees. Nor on cornstalks. Of the twenty-nine covered bridges that once graced the county, twenty-one have vanished.

The Sweet Shoppe, where we drank chocolate cokes (they seemed good then) and listened to Patsy Cline (who continues to seem plenty good to me), is gone, but you can still get fried mush for breakfast, which is better than it sounds, particularly on a cold winter's morning, and a pork tenderloin sandwich the size of a Frisbee which, with a cup of coffee provides all four of the basic food groups—calories, cholesterol, grease, and caffeine—and is tasty to boot.

Just up the road is Greenville, which anyone knows who is

familiar with *Annie Get Your Gun* (and if you're not you should be; it's splendid music) was the home of Annie Oakley. As a side note, Betty Hutton said that when she filmed the movie they soaked the local black walnuts in water and threw the water in her face to give her a dirty, woodsy stain—so besides being delicious, they were more versatile even than I thought, those walnuts.

Well to the east of Greenville is New Concord, Ohio. New Concord was the home of John Glenn. Glenn was rightly lionized as the first man in space. He also should have been horsewhipped for his part in the Keating Banking Scandal because *a)* he was a hero and *b)* he was a small town Ohio boy and so was taught better values than that, as any small town Ohio boy can tell you.

Yes, I know that sounds harsh but honestly now, if all those crooked bankers who were a part of that chicanery were stripped naked and forced to run a gauntlet of the investors (mostly older retirees) whom they swindled out of their life savings, don't you think the entire banking industry would be better as a result?

It is not just bankers, either, who could benefit from a little old prairie justice. There is so much brouhaha these days about energy shortages. I can't help but think that the board members of the utility companies and of their energy suppliers might be better for the occasional birch switch, administered by select customers (chosen, for the sake of fairness, by a lottery system). I would bet you every light bulb in China that we would soon have no energy shortage.

And while you are at it, if you emptied the rascals' pockets you would likely find the very profits that they insist have been lost and which are almost certainly only misplaced.

* * * * * * *

James Franciscus used to intone on television that "there are eight million stories in the Naked City." With all due apologies to the Big Apple, if you want stories, the small town is the place to find them.

Sodom and Gomorrah were small towns, after all. How do I know that, you ask? Simple. It is not nose count that defines the small town but rather the one inescapable fact of life: everyone knows everyone else's business. If you go back and read the Biblical story you will see that it was true in Sodom and it is no less true in Eaton, Ohio, nor ever was.

The history of Eaton comes complete with every sort of drama you could imagine and some you probably never thought of. Murders, scandals, incest, adultery, great love affairs, and heart-wrenching tragedy.

And Miss Ames. Miss Ames taught Social Studies—some history, some geography. Not very well, I'm afraid. She was a spinster, for reasons that I will get to in time, already old when I knew her and a bit frail. Her round face might have been cherubic but for the unfortunate fact of her whiskers. We laughed at those, particularly when, as sometimes happened, she would be unaware of the lint that had been caught in them. Children are cruel and I am afraid we lived up (or down) to that truism. It is a major step in growing up when you come to find that you are ashamed of the thoughtless hurt you inflicted on others when you were young. Some people never get to that regret. Some never even get to the awareness of it. Saddest of all, some never stop inflicting it.

Still, though we were sometimes cruel we were fond of the old dear in our childish fashion and tolerant of her foibles. Hers was a sad story in a romantic, Victorian way. Long years before, Miss Ames' younger brother had vanished. Just disappeared, leaving behind a wife and daughter. And a sister, obviously. Some thought him dead. Others theorized that he had been a victim of amnesia or had been shanghaied in some foreign port. Or perhaps there had been some secret, shameful act that had made it impossible for him to face those who loved him. We knew only that he was gone.

I hardly knew the wife and daughter, and how they responded to this strange disappearance I cannot say. But all of us were aware of Miss Ames' grief and her determination to solve the mystery.

It was for this reason that Miss Ames had never married, for her entire life had been devoted for several decades to searching for her brother. Her every penny, her every free hour, was spent in her search. She traveled often, following up any clue or hint, however tenuous, however distant. She read police reports, spent hours poring over old newspapers from throughout the country, even from foreign lands. An unidentified body, a wandering vagrant who could not remember his name, put her on a bus or a train, to New York, to Florida, to California. There were detectives, paid for with her scant earnings as a teacher. Phone calls, telegraphs, letters.

The years passed. The young, once pretty sister became an adult, the marriageable young woman became a spinster, the spinster an old, frail lady brushing lint from her whiskered chin and pretending not to hear her students snicker.

We watched her come and go. It was a romantic story, one of family devotion and untiring faith, doomed, it seemed, to have no end.

But end it did, though it was not Miss Ames' tireless efforts that brought it to conclusion. Rather it was the sudden, astonishing return of her errant brother and the even more astonishing explanation for his long absence. There was, it seemed, no tragedy, no mystery, no thrilling saga to impart. He had simply gone off, following his own restless spirit, and never thought to get in touch nor to return until his wife was gone, his daughter grown, his sister near the end of a long, fruitless life.

She welcomed the prodigal home, of course. How could she not, while the whole town watched, and for a brief time they could be seen together, brother and sister, daughter sometimes as well, chatting in low voices as they sat on her porch or strolled the town's streets in the twilight.

What did they speak of, one wondered? Did she berate him for his neglect? Did she speak in aggrieved tones of the trips, the search, the money and, oh, the years, the lost, long years, gone like the sunset fading into the darkening sky?

Did he regale her with tales of his adventures in distant lands, of long treks along dusty roads, of flights in balloons and flights of fancy, of villains and heroes and saints and great, great loves? Did they laugh together, cry together, argue, coax, plead, explain, pray?

She died not long after his return, perhaps bereft of her reason for living, and he drifted away once again, this time to be unmourned, unsought, undreamed of on long summer evenings.

Not a grand story, you understand, not the stuff of operas nor even of novels. In a big city, in New York or San Francisco or New Orleans, the years might have passed, the comings and going, all unnoticed, hers a lonely woman's private pain.

It was a small town thing.

(Excerpted from *Spine Intact, Some Creases*)

MOVING DAZE

The first time my friend George said, "You could live in West Virginia," I took it as rhetorical. I had been complaining about how I wanted to retire and devote myself to writing, and I couldn't, because without a job, I wouldn't have the income to allow me to continue to live in San Francisco. It's very difficult to afford to live in San Francisco *with* a job.

It wasn't until George called a few weeks later to reiterate his suggestion that I began to take it seriously.

"It's my great-grandparents' house, in Waltonsberg, next to mine," he said, "and I am sick of renting it out because it always gets trashed, and I don't want it just sitting empty, and of course I couldn't sell it."

"Well," I said, actually considering the possibility for the first time, "if you're sure."

"And you could take care of the garden, and see that things get done at both houses," he said. "So, really, you would be doing me a favor."

Putting it like that, I didn't see how I could refuse. I was not unaware that living in Waltonsberg, West Virginia, would be quite a change from living in San Francisco, and not only because West Virginia was in a part of the country that still had seasons, four of them, something San Francisco had long since given up on.

Still, I could afford to live in West Virginia even on my limited income, and the thought of being able to write full-time was too great a temptation to resist. He was having work done on the house—the last tenants really had trashed it, apparently—and we agreed that I would resign from my job as of the middle of September, and give notice of vacating my apartment effective the end of September, and arrive in Waltonsberg early in October, after a drive across country. I turned in my resignation at my job and gave my landlord thirty days notice on the apartment.

The first problem I had was that, hiring movers to transport my belongings all the way across country was going to cost me almost as much as continuing to live in San Francisco. I called a dozen or so moving companies for estimates, and their agents came with little hand-held computers, and sheets of regulations and estimates and talked of I.C.C. rules, and mentioned figures not too far off the national debt.

I quickly had to face reality: I would have to get rid of much of what I had accumulated in my twenty or so years in San Francisco. Well, all right, I am inclined to believe if you can't let something go, you don't own it, it owns you; and anyway, what do you really own? I mean, when you take the final trip, how much of it is going with you?

I went around the apartment, making lists, and becoming more ruthless with each circuit. I had to take the bed, and I couldn't bear to part with my books, at least most of them, and there were all those things you needed to set up housekeeping somewhere else, and which would surely cost me more to replace than to move. Still, I was able to reduce significantly the inventory of what I would ship.

Not, as it seemed, significantly enough. The estimates came down, but the lowest of them still represented a major piece of change for someone planning to retire and live on a very minor income.

I had just reached the stage of despair when I came upon one company that said they would do the move for the minimum figure, $1,000.00. This necessitated ridding myself of nearly all the furniture and most of my possessions, but it included moving the bed, which they would disassemble and reassemble at the new house, and twenty-six boxes.

That seemed like a fair number of boxes, except, as I explained, I had boxes in my possession that were six by ten inches, and one that was fifty-four by thirty, and surely they didn't mean that all boxes were created equal.

"Just so they fit in one thousand cubic feet of space in the moving van, along with the bed, is all that matters," the agent said, and he gave me a formula for calculating cubic feet, which involved height times width times depth, to which you added the year of my birth, and multiplied by the phases of the moon. I decided it was simpler to just envision how much of the interior of a moving van that must equal, and make a visual estimate as I packed the boxes.

I had a string of sidewalk sales, and people came in and out and bought furniture and oversized televisions which were too old to worry about moving, and some of the books, the ones to which I was least attached, and candy dishes and music CDs.

When I was done, and the apartment pretty well stripped, I started boxing up things. I made separate stacks: this could be disposed of, and this would probably go in the moving van, and this could go in the car I was going to rent to drive across country, a town car, I had decided, because their trunks are enormous and would carry much of what wouldn't fit in my thousand cubic feet in the moving van.

In the car-trunk pile, I put those things I knew I would need right away when I settled into the new house, like basic pots and pans, and the instant read meat thermometer, because I cannot tell if a roast is done by poking it with my finger the way Julia Child says to do, and if a roast gets overdone there isn't much you can do with it. I numbered each box as I packed it, and I kept a careful inventory by box numbers so I would know where everything was.

It was soon evident, however, even with the trunk of the car, and the sidewalk sales, and the people buying my furniture, that the boxes rapidly taking over the dining room were almost certainly more than would fit in my thousand cubic feet of moving van, as I envisioned them. I was going to have to rent a storage space and have some things shipped later.

I got a space for $150 a month, which I rented for four months, and it held 600 cubic feet of storage. I figured that was half of the space I was envisioning for the moving van, and another little bit on top of that. I rented a truck for two days, at $79 a day, and I paid a couple of day workers $20 each per day to help me move things, and I filled the storage locker on a Saturday afternoon and a Sunday morning.

A week before the end of September, when I had planned to vacate my apartment and start across country, George called to say that there had been some delays in the work he was having done on the house, and it wasn't going to be ready for me to move in until after the first of the year.

I had planned on stopping in my old home town in Ohio on my way across country, to visit family there, and when I talked to my niece, Karen, she said that her daughter, Maggie, who has a charming little house smack dab in the middle of a cornfield, was going to be taking a two month long trek through Asia with her fiancée, and her house would be empty from October through December, and she would be delighted to have me house-sit till she got back, so I called George back and said the delay was no problem, as I could stay at Maggie's and visit with family through Thanksgiving and Christmas.

When I began to pack the books, however, I could see that they represented a moving van on their own, as I have always been a book collector. I mentioned this to Maggie while we were working out details of my staying at her house, and she said that the cheapest way to move books was to box them up and mail them, and I could mail them to her if I liked. So, I began to pack books and take them one or two boxes at a time up to my local post office branch, and I numbered all the boxes and kept lists of them with postal receipts and inventories of their contents. I spent approximately $100 on postage and the necessary purchase of a few boxes and packing material.

By the end of the month, however, I had mailed about fifty

boxes, and I made several phone calls to Maggie to tell her they were on their way, and, worryingly, got no replies from her.

I also still had more than what I thought was going to fit in my thousand cubic feet of moving van, and my neighbor Lynette said, maybe we could put a few things in her closet, so we emptied out her closet and filled it with my overflow, and what we couldn't fit into the closet, we tucked here and there about her apartment, because probably, as she put it, no one would ever think to look behind her refrigerator or under her sofa, and we took her things to the house of her gentleman friend, who had to put some of his things in a small storage locker, which he rented for $30 a month, and which I said I would pay four months rent for.

I finally heard from Maggie, who had been visiting friends in New York and so was out of town since I had last talked to her, and she was a trifle dismayed to learn that there were fifty boxes of books waiting for her at her local post office, which the postman was unwilling to redeliver, and she had to rent a truck, which of course I paid for, which was $69 for the day, and she hired a couple of friends and gave them ten dollars each to help her move them all to her house, where they filled her second bedroom, and I sent her a check for $90 to offset her expenses.

I picked up the rental car, and Lynette helped me load it with the things I had to have with me, including my laptop so I could check my email on my way across country, and when we had crammed everything possible into the trunk of the car and the back seat and the front seat on the passenger's side, we still had a few boxes left over, and since her closet was already full, Lynette said why didn't we put them on the little balcony off her living room where she grew flowers, and we put a tarp over them, and set the plants on top of the tarp, and as she said, probably no one would notice at a casual glance, and I promised to arrange to have everything shipped to me as soon as I could.

The movers came the next morning and loaded my boxes and the bed into the moving van, and they charged me an extra $75 because they had to take the bed down a flight of stairs, and another $35 for packing materials, because I had left my crystal for them to pack, thinking that was safest, and an extra $120 because it took them overtime to load everything into the truck, as they had to park some distance away and go up and down the outside stairs without an elevator to use. When they were done, they informed me that I still had nearly half of my allotted space left, and I suggested packing up the things in the trunk of the car, which would free up the car's interior, but they explained that it would cost me extra to have them unload everything from the car and reload it in the truck, and as much of that wasn't even boxed up, they would have to charge me, too, for boxing it, plus the additional packing materials, so we left things as they were, as my expenses were already mounting.

It took me a couple of days longer to drive across country than I had anticipated because, as loaded as it was, the car did not go up mountains as spiritedly as one would like, which meant another $300-$400 in meals and motel expenses, and my mileage was considerably less than I had estimated. Also, because it is not safe to let a car sit in a parking lot overnight with the back seat and the passenger's seat filled with boxes, I had to unpack those things each night and repack them each morning, which took up extra time.

When I got to Ohio, I found that Maggie's Asia trek had been delayed, and she would not be leaving for two weeks. My rental car was due back in two days, and there was a problem about what to do with all the things in the trunk and the back seat and the passenger's seat in front, as Maggie's spare bedroom was now filled floor to ceiling with boxes of books.

I rented a small storage locker for $99 a month, for three months, and put most of what I had brought in that, except for my clothes and the laptop, which I hadn't been able to use anyway coming across country, as I never could get on the Internet, and I had to go to the local library when I arrived to check my email on their computer.

What wouldn't fit into the little storage locker, we fitted into Karen's closet, and she took her things from the closet over to her mother's house, and her mother found some room in her storage shed, and in the trunk of her car, and I promised her that I would arrange to have them shipped as quickly as possible.

Shortly after Christmas, Karen and her sister, Becky, moved me from Ohio to West Virginia in Becky's van, which we loaded with the things from the little storage locker, and the books from Maggie's, except that we couldn't quite fit them all in, and I left a half dozen boxes and a note for Maggie that I would retrieve them at the first opportunity, and the things that were in Karen's closet I left, with the promise to get them as soon as I could.

When we got to George's, the new house still wasn't ready for me to move in, and George said he thought the best thing was for me to stay at his house until the other one was ready, so we put most of my things in a spare bedroom in what would be my house, because that room was finished already, and the rest of my things went into the attic in George's house, and by this time the movers had arrived with the van and they unloaded everything into that spare bedroom in my house, and set up the bed, and what we couldn't find room for, I put into a small storage locker that I rented locally for $59 a month, for three months.

It was February before I was able to move into my house, and I then discovered that I must have packed all my inventory lists in one of the boxes somewhere, only I never could find which box, since I had boxes at Lynette's in San Francisco, and at Karen's in Ohio, and Maggie's in the cornfield, and in George's attic and the storage locker at Waltonsberg, not to mention the ones the movers had unloaded in the new house, which I was unpacking one by one.

My problem is: where is the little instant read meat thermometer, as I would really like to fix a rib roast for my very first dinner in my new home, and I never could tell whether a roast was done by poking it with my finger the way Julia Child does?

LOVE IN THE RIGHT LIGHT

Afterward, Linda thought she ought to have known what kind of day it would be. If practically the first thing you see when you go out to pick up the morning paper is a head without a body scurrying across the street, what kind of a day *could* it be?

Of course, it wasn't really a bodiless head. She wasn't that silly. It was a cat or a possum or even a piece of litter, and a trick of the early morning light and the lingering remnants of sleep, not yet dispelled by a cup of coffee. Still, as an omen, it was pretty significant. Only, she couldn't tell Jason about it. Her husband already thought she was daft. There was no point in giving him any additional ammunition for his daily tirades on her eccentricity. Heaven knew, he had enough to work with already.

She ought to have known, for instance, the minute she picked up the phone and heard Annabelle's voice. Annabelle was not one of those people who called without a reason, just to chat, the way Linda herself often did. If Annabelle went to the trouble to pick up the telephone and punch in seven numbers in succession, you could bet money on it, she wanted something from you.

Linda always forgot that, because she was always so delighted to hear Annabelle's voice. In her excitement, she never remembered that other until it had been sprung on her.

"I've been thinking about the reunion," Annabelle said. That ought to have been another warning. Annabelle was in charge of the planning for their fifty-year high school reunion. Linda had been happy about it for her, because Annabelle just thrived on organizing things; unlike Linda herself, who always seemed to be chasing her own tail, as Jason never tired of telling her.

"I just know everything's going to be perfect, with you in charge," Linda said in all innocence.

"Well, it's been a lot of work. The fifty-year class is a big deal, you know, so I want everything to be just right. Otherwise, they'll just think we're a bunch of doddering old idiots."

"And it will be, absolutely perfect, I just know it will," Linda gushed, and then she made one of those mistakes that Jason liked to point out to her. "Linda," he would say, in that infinitely patient voice of his, "how could you not see that one coming?"

What she said next was, "So, what have you got planned?"

"I'm so glad you asked me that," Annabelle said, "because that's exactly why I am calling you. I want you to sing."

For a minute, Linda actually thought she might have heard wrong. "To sing? Sing what? I don't sing any more, not in ages."

"Well, you used to sing all the time. I remember your singing 'Ciriciribim'. You sounded just like Jane Powell."

"She hasn't sung in ages either," Linda said, not entirely sure how Jane Powell had gotten into this; but at least that point she was prepared to deal with. "I read this interview with her just a couple of months ago, in *People* magazine. She said she had no voice left, not for years. Because she didn't sing right. She said they taught her right, at MGM, how to sing from the diaphragm and breath and everything, but then when she got into the studio, she'd just sing her usual old anyway, and now she doesn't have any voice. And I don't either, I'm sure." She paused and then, thinking she hadn't made herself clear enough, she added, before Annabelle could say anything, "not that I would actually know. It's been ages since I sang a single note."

"You told me you sang in the church choir." Annabelle's tone was accusing, as if Linda were attempting some sort of deception.

"Well, that's a lot different from 'Ciriciribim', with all those high notes. And besides, I haven't done that for a good ten, fifteen years either. Honestly...what were you thinking I would sing, anyway? People don't really sing at high school reunions, do they? I don't remember any singing at the last one."

"But we're the fifty year class, which makes us special. They told me I could arrange things however I wanted them, as long as I stayed within the ten-minute time frame. And I thought it would be nice, if we did the same things we did at our prom, I thought that would be lovely."

"At our prom?" Linda thought for a moment.

"Yes. And you sang at that, remember?"

"I sang 'I Love You Truly' at our prom."

"That's right. And it was wonderful, I remember sitting there with tears in my eyes through the whole song."

"Annabelle, you can't sing 'I Love You Truly' at a school reunion. It's not a reunion kind of song."

"Well, if you want to be technical, it's not a prom kind of song, either, was it?"

"I sang it for Jason. It was the first time he had ever been exposed to our gang, and I wanted to make him feel welcome. Plus, it's a wedding song, I was making, like, you know, a statement."

"Isn't Jason going to be at the reunion with you?"

Linda could already feel the ground slipping away under her, the way it did sometimes when you tried to put your foot down, and there was nothing there to put it on. "Yes, I suppose he is, although he hasn't exactly said so. But...."

"Well, then."

"Annabelle, there must be people from our glass who still do sing, in church, or—what about Bobby Montgomery, didn't he used to sing in a band? Wouldn't that be so much nicer, if you must have singing at the reunion, to have an actual professional like Bobby Montgomery."

"Linda, Bobby Montgomery has left us, don't you remember? Eight years ago. He ran his car into a herd of cows. Drunk.

Bobby, I mean, not the cows."

"Oh." Which left Linda feeling completely at a loss, and even a shade guilty, for invoking the name of someone who had died in a cow accident. It almost seemed like thumbing your nose at life's fallibilities. "Well, but surely, someone sings," she said lamely.

"But, don't you see, it wouldn't be the same. You were *our* singer, you sang for everything, parties and celebrations and the Christmas concert every year. We all looked up to you so."

"I didn't realize anybody looked up to me especially."

"Well, of course we did, silly, everyone practically worshipped you. You were the only one who took tap *and* baton. And the way you sang, like an angel."

Linda sighed. You couldn't have someone talk about worshipping you and be nitpicky about singing a single song. "Okay, I guess I could sing something. But not 'I Love You Truly.' Honestly, I would feel like a fool."

"Anything, then, just so it's from the fifties. What else did they sing in the fifties? Who was popular?"

"Rosemary Clooney? I can't sing 'Mambo Italiano' either."

"What about Patti Page?"

"'How Much Is the Doggie in the Window'?"

"She sang 'Tennessee Waltz'."

"How would that sound at a Waltonsberg, West Virginia school reunion? It would sound ridiculous. People would laugh if I sang 'Tennessee Waltz'."

"Well, you'll think of something. Just let me know so I can tell Norma Jean; she's going to accompany you. She's going to play 'Pomp and Circumstance', too."

"'Pomp and Circumstance'? At the alumna?"

"Linda," Annabelle said, all tested patience, "it's a celebration of our class, of our graduation. That is what they played when we graduated, if you will remember."

Linda felt when she had hung up not so much as if she had agreed, but more like she had run out of ways to disagree, like she did with Jason. Even when she had marshaled all her arguments beforehand, he somehow managed to negate all of them until finally they just ran out and she was left with nothing more to say. This way, ad lib, she ought to have known from the start that she didn't stand a chance; not when Annabelle had her mind set on something.

It wasn't any better when Norma Jean called right afterward, either.

"I don't have any idea what I'm going to sing," Linda explained wearily. "I can't imagine how she ever talked me into this. Or you, either, for that matter. Are you really going to play 'Pomp and Circumstance'?"

"Well, you know how Annabelle is, once she gets her mind set on something."

"Exactly," Linda said, thinking of all the times Annabelle had steamrolled them into doing things they didn't want to do. "Remember her wedding? Anybody else would have given up and eloped. She had no one to give her away, and just this one bridesmaid. Who was she? This little fat girl, plain as mud, in that hot pink dress, she looked like someone had sprayed the Goodyear Blimp."

"That was me," Norma Jean said.

"No, no, it wasn't the bridesmaid, now that I recall...." Linda paused and thought for a moment. "No, it was that other girl, I remember her clearly now."

"There wasn't any other girl. I was the only bridesmaid, and we didn't have a flower girl. There was nobody but me and Annabelle."

"Well, now that I think of it, she wasn't a bridesmaid. Maybe she came with someone. And her dress wasn't pink, it was yellow, I can see it now, but I can't for the life of me think who she was. Nobody from our class, though, I'm sure of that. Oh, I remember, she was a cousin of Roger's, or something like that."

When she had hung up on a decidedly cool Norma Jean, Linda poured herself a cup of coffee and went to stand at the back door. The coffee was bitter, stale. She poured sugar into it directly from the sugar-bowl, got the milk from the refrigerator and poured it into the cup until the coffee was almost white. Now it was barely lukewarm, and just as bitter underneath the milk and sugar, but she went back to the door and sipped at it anyway, gazing out through the screen door at the long, narrow back yard.

She thought about how her husband was going to react to this. Oh, Lord, he will think it's a big joke, she thought dismally. He thought practically everything she did was a big joke. Worse, he would see in it the confirmation, once again, of his opinion of her as the living incarnation of Lucy Ricardo. Despite what she had told Annabelle, he hadn't yet actually agreed that he was going to the reunion with her; and he almost certainly wouldn't if he heard about this singing business.

She could hear him already. "Linda, I swear, you just never have learned to say no to anyone, and now you're going to get up and make a fool of yourself in front of all your old classmates, and I am expected to sit there and watch."

A bird in the big pear tree called "Video, video, video," over and over in those endless triads. She had always meant to learn the different birdcalls. She had even bought a book at Barnes and Noble, with what must be a hundred or so pictures of different birds, many of which looked identical as near as she could tell, and it described all their different calls, only she didn't recognize any of them the way they were written.

Really, it was difficult, practically impossible, wasn't it, to describe sounds in words, particularly anything so different as bird songs. Probably the words the writer used were what the songs sounded like to him, but none of them sounded like what she was used to hearing from her backyard. Nowhere, for instance, did he mention "video, video, video." Or, "pretty, pretty, pretty," which she heard every day from the pear tree, and she hadn't the slightest idea which of the birds it was. And she really would like to know—it was why she had bought the book in the first place—what a cardinal sounded like, but the book was absolutely no help with that. According to it, the cardinal sat out there calling "what cheer, what cheer, what cheer;" but she had never heard anything that sounded like that, and certainly there were cardinals out there, and unless they were mute, they must say something to one another. Birds had to communicate, didn't they? But if you didn't know someone's language, you were just left out, weren't you?

So, then, what had they sung in the fifties? 'Jailhouse Rock'. 'Love Me Tender'. 'Rock around the Clock'. 'Love Is a Many Splendored Thing'. They were all rock 'n' roll, or about love, weren't they? She remembered singing with the other girls, all those silly love songs with lyrics that didn't come anywhere close to what it turned out love and marriage was all about. She might as well do that theme song from Ruby Gentry. The popular version had been instrumental, but there were lyrics to it too, she had heard them somewhere or other.

Ruby, something, something, something.... She thought of Jennifer Jones in those tight jeans, and began to gyrate her hips, humming the melody to herself while she tried to think of the words.

"What's the matter?" her husband said from behind her.

She turned around, embarrassed. She hunched her shoulders, shook her head, trying to make the hip gyrations part of some larger, more complicated movement. "What do you mean, what's the matter?"

"Well, the way you're squirming about, it looked like you'd gotten a bee in your britches or something."

"You don't have to stay and watch," she said sharply.

"It's been a quiet day," he said, dropping into one of the kitchen chairs. "I might as well."

"Fine, you can just sit there all morning," she said, "I have laundry to do."

"You just did laundry yesterday," he pointed out.

"You think there isn't more by today? I don't know how you manage; you must just take all your clothes out of the closet and drag them around the back yard." She went through to the laundry room. There was nothing in the hamper but one pair of socks and some boxer shorts. She threw them into the washer and started the water running anyway.

Dull. That was Jason, there was just no denying it: Jason was dull. Oh, he had been a good husband all these many years, and a good provider, and he was a good father to their two sons, who were grown up themselves now. If they were here there'd be plenty enough laundry accumulated, even in one day. Jason just wasn't doing his share, if you wanted to look at it like that.

If she were to make up a full inventory of the man to whom she had been married those forty-six years, she knew there was much she could put in the assets column, and not so very much to put under liabilities.

Dull, however, would have to go there. And the fact that he just never did seem to understand her, not her particular most personal needs and feelings. After all these years, for instance, he still got impatient with her when she cried watching a movie, or tried to get him to understand why she was all excited about a poem, and although he denied it whenever she challenged him, she knew that he really did not care for the flowers that she liked to have all over the house, little bunches of daisies or pansies in jelly glasses, because every time she bought a really pretty vase, it somehow managed to get itself broken within a week or two. He always blamed her for that, too, though she herself was convinced it was some malignant spirit that had long ago set itself to torment her in that particular fashion.

Some men, on the other hand, liked flowers, and poetry, and tearful movies. Victor did. They had shared long, meaningful conversations on just such subjects years and years ago, when they had been in high school together, and over the years, when they exchanged the occasional letter or Christmas card note, he often included snippets of poetry, so she knew his interests hadn't changed.

Nor, she felt certain, had his longing for her. She had always known that he loved her, silently and from afar, though never once had he declared his love. Of course, she hadn't taken him seriously, and besides, it was Jason that she had loved in that way, the getting married way; but she had privately always cherished Victor's adulation.

Which was why, when he called to say he was in town for the class reunion, and could she have lunch with him, as there was something he really wanted to tell her, she jumped at the opportunity. Particularly when he hemmed and hawed a bit before saying, "Do you think it would be all right if it was, like, just the two of us? I mean, would Jason mind?"

"Mind? Heavens, I'm sure he would be quite happy to be spared all that old nostalgia about our high school days," she told him.

She was quite certain, too, that she knew what it was he wanted to tell her, and she spent a good while thinking how she felt about it. It had been many years since a man told her he loved her. It had been years, in fact, since Jason had told her, in those exact words, that he loved her, and certainly she had never been in a situation since she had married him when another man might tell her that.

Well, it wasn't as if she meant to run off with Victor, after all. It was one thing to fantasize a torrid affair, she supposed every married woman did that at some time in her life, but it was quite another to actually contemplate doing it, and she was not; but, still, wasn't it going to be nice for the ego when, after all these years, he finally got around to declaring his love.

She spent a great deal of time rehearsing just how she was going to respond. Graciously, of course, and openly flattered; but she would have to be firm. She was a married woman, a mother, a member of her church and her community. He must be made to understand that nothing could come of it.

On the other hand, she must let him know that she would always be pleased to know that his love for her continued unabated. Certainly she didn't want it to end.

She took great pains in dressing for lunch, at the Lucky Pierre Room. She already had an appointment that morning to have her hair done for the banquet, and she applied her makeup with special care.

Jason whistled when he saw her. "Looking good," he said.

"Any special occasion?"

"Lunch with Victor. I told you he was in town." She paused and, deliberately tempting fate, added, "Want to join us?"

He gave a little half laugh, the way he did when he was sure whatever she had said wasn't meant to be taken seriously. It never failed to annoy her. "No, you go ahead and have fun."

"I mean to," she said, just a trifle coolly. She wondered what he would say if she told him the point of this little luncheon. Would he be jealous?

Probably not. That was the problem with a husband of long standing: they tended to take you for granted. Well, maybe she would just have something to surprise him with in the near future. When it was over and Victor was gone, she would tell him exactly how another man felt about her, someone who did not take her for granted. And let him put that in his pipe and smoke it.

* * * * * *

Victor was already there when she arrived at the restaurant. He stood up when he saw her making her way across the room. He had always been the epitome of politeness, and she had to admit, he looked good. He never seemed to age, or hardly at all. Jason had lost practically all of his hair and he was a good twenty pounds overweight, and much of that was at his waist-line. Victor was as slim-waisted as he had been in high school, and he had a full head of hair, and of course he had always dressed beautifully, unlike Jason, who sometimes looked as if he had fled a burning building.

He kissed her cheek and helped her with her chair, and when the waiter appeared ordered her a sherry, which was what she used to drink, although she hadn't had one in years. He was drinking a martini, and she rather thought she would have liked to try one of those, but she didn't want to spoil the occasion by seeming fussy.

The draperies were open at the windows, the room bathed

in sunlight. She wished after all that she had suggested cock-tails instead of lunch. That made for a much more romantic setting, didn't it? And by then it would have been evening, and the lighting would have been so much more flattering to her. All this sunlight, it didn't seem appropriate, really, for the moment, and it was bound to show up every line and shadow in her face, when she wanted him to see her as he had seen her all those years ago.

She had an uncomfortable thought. Victor looked so very young, really, and she knew perfectly well that this light wasn't doing anything for her—what if people thought she was his mother. She looked around, but no one seemed to be staring at them.

They made small talk until her sherry came, catching up on some of their old classmates. After a few moments, the conver-sation petered out. She thought of prompting him, but decided against it. If he really did intend to tell her, finally, how he felt about her, it ought to be all his doing, and no machination of hers.

He cleared his throat finally, and took a large sip of his martini, and set it aside decisively. "There's something I have to tell you," he said. "I've been wanting to tell you this for years, but, well, it just never seemed to be the right time, or there were other people around—I couldn't very well say this to you with Jason on hand." He laughed just a shade nervously.

This is it, then, she thought, her heart beating just a little faster. His declaration of love, after decades of worshiping her in silence and from afar. No, of course he couldn't make that confession with Jason there.

Of course, she would have to tell Jason all about it. You couldn't have another man tell you he was in love with you, had been in love with you his whole life, and simply not mention that to your husband. It was practically faithless.

She sipped her sherry—really, it was hard to imagine that she had once liked it, it tasted downright cloying to her now—and tried to think how she was going to break the news to Jason.

He was certain to be shocked, probably angry. Well, it served him right, all these years of taking her for granted. It would be a good thing for him to know that other men didn't.

Victor was looking expectantly at her, as if waiting for some response. She wasn't sure what she was supposed to say. He was the one doing the saying, wasn't he? "Yes?" she prompted him.

"I hope you take this the right way," he said.

She gave him what she thought of as her gracious smile, accompanied by a flutter of her eyelashes, which she had rehearsed in her mirror for much of the morning, until Jason saw her and asked if she had something in her eye. "I don't suppose there are too many different ways to take it," she said.

"Well, people react differently."

People? What an odd choice of words. How many different people had he made protestations of love to, for Heaven's sake? It wasn't a group sort of announcement, it seemed to her. She let her gracious smile fade just a little and stilled her eyelashes. Hopefully he did not think she was the sort of woman who would welcome being "I Pluribus Unum."

"I'm gay," he said.

She blinked, trying to take that in, and for the moment finding that she couldn't assimilate it.

"Homosexual," he said, staring at her as if he thought she might not understand.

"I know what it means," she said; but she didn't understand, either. How could he be in love with her, and homosexual; that didn't make any sense? What could he mean?

"I've always wanted to tell you. I thought maybe you already knew. Some of the others from our class do, I'm sure, and I thought, well, we're all going to be getting together, and there's always lots of gossip about one another, and I didn't want you to hear about this from somebody else. I mean, we've been friends since first grade, I thought I ought to be honest with you, you know."

"Well, of course," she said, feeling utterly chagrined. He wasn't in love with her; that was what he meant. She said, stupidly, "I thought you loved me."

"Oh, I do," he said quickly, fervently, "I've always thought the world of you, I even, when we were kids, well, I had this crush on you."

"But you just said you're gay."

"Yes, but, I wasn't then, when we were nine, ten years old. Oh, I suppose I was, but I hadn't figured it out, yet, you see, you don't usually get it sorted out till you are in your teens, or even later. I have a friend in Los Angeles, he didn't realize until he was twenty-two. Up till then, he had been entirely celibate, no girls or boys, no one, and then he got to thinking, and he called up this friend he had that he knew was gay, and he said he sort of thought maybe he was too, and he thought he would like to try, well, you know, doing it with someone, to find out, and when they did, then he knew for certain, just like that, and he's been gay ever since. I mean, he's just about the gayest person I know, but not until he was twenty-two."

"Well, I'm very happy for him, I'm sure," she said, at a loss as to how he thought any of that would interest her. Certainly she didn't want to know what it was that people like that did with one another, at any age.

"But I knew long before that," he said. "Like, when I was fifteen, there was this older man, a teacher, to tell you the truth. You're not shocked, are you? Or disgusted, or anything like that?"

"Well, it is something of a shock, of course," she said. "I mean, each to his own, is what I always say. It's just, well, it takes some getting used to." She thought for a moment, the rest of what he had said sinking in finally. "A teacher? You don't mean Mister Carmen?"

"I shouldn't have told you that," he said, shamefaced. "It wasn't like you think, though. I mean, he didn't molest me, or anything."

"But, you were a mere child, and he was a grown-up. No wonder you got this silly idea in your head, that you were homosexual, it was just him making you think that way."

"But he didn't. Make me think that way, I mean. I already did think that way. By then I was noticing the other boys in gym, stuff like that."

"Well, the other boys, that's something different, but a grown man. Probably if he hadn't molested you, you would have grown up to be perfectly normal. You might have fallen in love with a girl and gotten married and had a family, just like everyone else does."

"I wouldn't have, though. I mean, I like women well enough, I have lots of good friends who are women, but I couldn't fall in love with one, not that way."

"But you already said, you had a crush on me," she practically wailed. A woman at the next table glanced in their direction, but Linda gave her a frosty look and she quickly returned her attention to her own lunch. "You did say you had a crush on me," she said more calmly.

"I did. I still do, in a way," Victor said.

"So?"

"It's just not a romantic way. You know, sexual. I would never think of you that way."

She sniffed. "Well, no, of course not. I would never think of you that way either. Maybe some other woman could have changed your mind, though, someone prettier than me, or sexier, or, well, more to your liking."

"There wasn't anyone prettier than you," he said with a little laugh that riled her all the more. "Still isn't, and you are entirely to my liking, but, well," he shrugged. "You're a woman."

"I'm glad at least you noticed that fact." She looked long and hard at him and realized out of the blue that he was wearing a hairpiece. She had never seen that before. It was the light in the room that made it apparent. Good Heavens, maybe he was as bald as Jason. She thought about his slim waistline, and looked at the way he was sitting, and wondered if he might be wearing a corset.

Despite herself, she giggled aloud.

* * * * * * *

Jason was working a crossword puzzle when she got home. She put her purse on the hall console and set her hat beside it, and came right out with it.

"I just found out that Victor is gay," she said. "And, he wears a hairpiece."

"Victor? You mean that writer guy? The one you were having lunch with?"

"Well, how many Victors do we know, I ask you? And the one we do know is homosexual, as it turns out."

"Well, I knew that. I thought you did, too."

"Oh, don't be ridiculous, how could you have known that, I just found it out myself?" A sudden thought crossed her mind. "Oh, you're not trying to tell me, are you, that, he, well...?"

"He what?" he asked without even looking up from the puzzle.

"You know, to you?"

"Came on to me? Linda, don't be silly, I've seen Victor, what, two, maybe three times in my life, and you were sitting right there both times."

"Well, then how can you say you knew this?"

He shrugged. "Guys can just tell sometimes, is all. You just know."

"Oh, great. So you knew this all along, since we've been married, I suppose is what you are saying, and you never said a word to me."

"Well, but why would I? It's not like it's any of our business, is it? Why do you care anyway? What's it got to do with us?"

"Nothing, but it strikes me as peculiar, to say the least, that it never occurred to you to say to me, your wife, as it happens, to say some time in passing, oh, by the way, you know that Victor, the one you have known your entire life and practically grew up with, he's a homosexual."

"No, it never did occur to me, and I can't imagine what you are all in a lather about now, for Pete's sake.

"I am not in a lather, it's just that it seems odd to me that you considered this so inconsequential our whole lives and now you are making this big deal over it."

"Linda, I'm not making a big deal out of it, I could care less whether he gets it on with men, women, or goats."

"You don't have to get vulgar."

"It's of absolutely no interest to me, okay?"

"Fine, then let's just drop the subject."

"I guess now you're going to have one of your sulks?" he asked.

"I don't have sulks, as you put it," she snapped.

He chuckled, in that maddening way. Really, one day she might just throttle him. He wrote something into his crossword puzzle, paused a moment, and asked, "Who wrote, 'grow old along with me'? Was that Browning?"

She had to think for a moment. "Grow old along with me, ta da, ta da, ta da. I used to know that."

"'Grow old along with me, the best is yet to be'," he surprised her by reciting; she had never known him to remember any poetry, "'the last of life for which the first was made'."

"The best is yet to be?" she said, with a snort of disdain. "Did Mister Grow-Old-Along-with-Me find anything to rhyme with heartburn? Or arthritis?" She screwed up her face thoughtfully. "Hmm, I guess you could do something with constipation and indignation, if you worked at it."

To her annoyance, he laughed aloud. "Linda, you don't have arthritis...."

"I most certainly do, I just don't trumpet my every misery the way some people do."

"...Or constipation either, for that matter."

"Oh, really? And how pray would you know whether I have constipation or not, may I ask?"

He chuckled more quietly. "How would I know? We share a bathroom, Sweetheart, you know, that little room right off of our bedroom."

"Are you telling me that you lie in bed and listen to me using the bathroom? That is the most disgusting thing I have ever heard."

"We are talking about normal, healthy bodily functions. If I happen to hear my wife taking a poop in the next room, there is nothing disgusting about it."

She gave him a frosty look. "Sometimes I don't think I know you at all," she said.

"Sometimes it seems to me like you never did," he said.

"Well, I could say the same thing, you have always been totally ignorant of what I am really like."

"Am not."

"Are too," she said, but then even she had to giggle at the silliness of their discussion, you could hardly call it a quarrel, about something as inane as her using the bathroom. She went to the window and looked out at the pear tree. Oddly, she found herself thinking about Victor's hairpiece. Something about the color of it had teased at her mind, and all of a sudden she knew what it was: it was the same color as her pet rabbit's fur had been years ago.

"Do you remember Puff?" she asked entirely out of the blue, but Jason never seemed to have any trouble keeping up with those dramatic leaps she made from one subject to another.

"Was that the little gray dog?"

"No, that was Bonnie Doone, and she wasn't gray, she was off-white. Puff was my rabbit."

"Oh, yes, I remember now, fawn-colored."

"That's her. I decided one day it wasn't fair, her being cooped up like that in a cage, so I set her free, out on the back porch. I thought she could have the whole yard to play in and, for a rabbit, that would be just heaven. And the neighbor's cat killed her, that big, mean old tom from next door, I chased him under their porch with a broom, I tried for an hour or more to get at him under there, till Mrs. Markey came out and told me to go home before she called my mom."

"The point being?" he asked, finally looking up from his crossword.

"The point being, it's funny, all those things you let go of, or they let go of you, and you never quite realize at the time that that's it, they're gone forever, and someday you're going to wish you could get them back, but you never can, quite."

She turned from the window and studied this quiet, maddening man to whom she was so very married. She felt altogether at sea. Hairpieces and corsets and men in love with other men—not that there was anything wrong with that, except when you thought they were in love with you. She should have known, she thought, when she saw that head scurrying across the street first thing this morning.

"Oh, Jason, how do other people always manage to get things right, and I always seem to be on the wrong boat?"

"You're on the right boat. You're on the boat with me, aren't you?" He put his puzzle aside and got up and came to where she was standing, and took her in his arms.

She leaned against him. He *was* comfortable; and maybe it wasn't twenty pounds overweight; now that she thought about it, ten was probably closer to the truth, and really, baldness could be kind of sexy in a man, couldn't it, just think about Yul Brynner, for heaven's sake. "Yes," she said, "but there's no point pretending, you think I'm a perfect fool."

"Now, you've got that half right," he said. "I think you're perfect."

Of course, it wasn't quite the same as saying, in so many words, "I love you." Still, it wasn't so very bad, either, for a man who had never been particularly romantic.

"What are you going to sing at the reunion?" he asked unexpectedly. She hadn't even known that he knew about that, but she wasn't terribly surprised. He always seemed to know about everything. Where she was concerned, anyway.

"'I Love You Truly'," she said.

He gave her a bemused look. "At a school reunion?"

"It's a statement," she said.

LOAVES AND FISHES

Wilbur's life wasn't all that bad, as a goldfish's life went. He hated waiting for food, of course. It had been better when the man was there. The woman sometimes went for days at a time without dropping the little flakes into the bowl, and she never made funny faces at him through the glass, or tickled the surface of the water with her fingers, as the man used to do.

Still, there was no goldfish garden in the bowl, and no gold-fish grocery store, and there was little that he could do but wait, and think, as he often did, how much he wanted a companion. He dreamed of that often, and wished for it, and he had even selected a name already for the friend that he was sure would join him one day: Orville, in honor of that legend of the two goldfish who learned to fly.

"Company is fine," the Old Fish used to tell him, "and the best is your own." Which was fine for an oldster like him, who lived in an enormous aquarium with all kinds of company, and not in a glass bowl by himself.

Still, Wilbur's life wasn't all that bad. There was the little ceramic mermaid, who blew bubbles out her mouth, and made the water sweet and ticklish for him, and there was the castle, with the opening in the middle, so he could swim right through it, and then it was through the fronds, thick enough a body could hide in them, and back to the mermaid, and by the time he got to the castle again, he had forgotten all about it, and was delighted anew each time. When he dreamed of his future companion, of Orville, he could hardly wait to show Orville the castle, and the bubbling mermaid, and the frond garden.

In the meantime, though, he had to wait to eat, and Orville was still only a wish that he made each day on the seaweed, as he had been taught to do. Outside, he could see the woman working in her kitchen, and he swam in tight little circles, waving his fins and hoping to catch her attention.

* * * * * * *

She was entirely aware of the goldfish in his bowl, swimming frantically. She knew perfectly well that he was hungry—she hadn't fed him in, what, three days now? She supposed she would have to give him something today. She didn't want him to die, just to suffer, the way she had suffered when her husband died, and she no longer had him to punish for marrying her.

She was making a fish stew, the kitchen already filled with the aroma of tomatoes simmering, and garlic and onions, and blended with it the scent of the loaves baking in the oven, that were just about ready by this time. She would eat well. She always did, though she had made a habit of being parsimonious with her husband, until he had cheated her of that little pleasure.

She was about to add the cod to the stew when the knock at the kitchen door startled her so badly she nearly dropped the fish on the floor. She wiped her hands carelessly on her apron and went to the door.

It was one of those bums, Okies, they called them, though they were not all of them from Oklahoma. Times were hard. There were many people on the road. She couldn't imagine why. What did they think would be different somewhere else? A loser was a loser, wasn't he? Location didn't change anything.

"I was wondering," he said, and she could see his nostrils catch the scent of that fish stew, and flare perceptibly, "if I could maybe swap some work for some food. I am powerful hungry. It's been three days, now. Anything you could spare."

She was about to slam the door in his face—why people like him thought they had the right to bother decent people like her, was beyond her ken—when she thought about that pile of firewood in the back yard. She had haggled old Jackson down to half what he had asked for to start, but he had left it in a great big jumble, refusing to put it in the woodshed for her, and she could see at a glance that some of the logs were too big.

"There's some wood to be cut and stacked," she said. "If you've a mind to see to that, I could give you a bowl of fish stew when you're finished, and a loaf of bread."

She could all but hear him groan inwardly when he looked at the stack of wood. It would take a good hour of hard work, even for a sturdy, healthy man, and he looked pretty weakly. She fixed a steely eye on him when he appeared about to argue, and he looked away from her, and down at the ground, and back at the wood. His shoulders slumped.

"I can't use anything longer than twenty inches," she said, "so you will have to cut everything down to size, and then it goes in the woodshed, there. Stacked neat, mind you."

"You got an axe?" he asked.

"It's in the shed," she said, and left him to it, and went back to the kitchen.

* * * * * *

She heard him later at the pump, washing up, and looked out the window to check on him. The wood was all gone. She could see it through the open door of the woodshed. It was no more than three quarters of an hour since he had started, which made her believe that she had been too easy on him. When he showed up in the kitchen doorway, wiping his hands on the legs of his pants, she said, "There is all that dead shrubs need to be cleared out of the garden there, if you would just bag all that up, and set it out front."

"I was expecting to get my lunch now," he said, not so much belligerent as plaintive.

"When the work is done," she said, and turned her back on him. He stood where he was for a moment and then, with a sigh, went away again, and she saw out the window that he had gone to work on the dead bushes.

The bread was done now, the loaves toasted to that nutmeg brownness, and beautifully risen, except for a couple of puny little ones, where she had run short on dough. She set them out to cool, and picked the poorest one of them, and set that on a plate on the table for him, when he came in to eat.

When the stew was finished, she spooned a scant ladleful into a bowl, and set that beside the bread. Only, the oddest thing, she must have mixed the loaves up, because the one on the table was the biggest, fattest of them all. She put it on the sill with the others, where they were cooling and got the smallest, driest-looking one of them, and put that on his plate instead, and saw that she had, after all, filled his bowl too full, it was clear up to the brim.

She dumped that back into the pot on the stove, and this time, was very careful to put no more than a single ladle of the stew into the bowl, so that it barely covered the bottom. After all, she was giving him a whole loaf of bread, wasn't she? There was no need to be over-generous with the stew.

To her surprise, he appeared at the kitchen door just as she was setting the bowl back on the table.

"I will have my lunch, now," he said.

"When the labor is done," she said smartly, and went to look out the window, meaning to let him have it over the unfinished work—only, it wasn't unfinished, the garden had been cleaned of dead shrubs, and when she stuck her head out to look, she saw the neat bundles of them, all tied up, waiting at the front of the house for the garbage collection.

Really, it was like magic, she had never known anyone to work so fast in her whole life. It would have taken her departed husband half the day to do this much, and it wouldn't have been done so well. She was so disconcerted that, try though she might, she could not think of anything else to tax the stranger with.

"Well, all right, then, come on in," she said in a voice that begrudged the welcome.

He came in and she motioned him toward the table, but as she did so, she saw that she had once again filled his bowl too full, and before he could even sit down at the table, she snatched it up, and emptied it once more into the pot, and ladled the stew back into it even more skimpily than before.

She brought it back to the table, and as she did, she realized that while her back was turned, he must have swapped that little loaf of bread for one of the better ones, and it made her angry, him trying to pull a stunt like that on her, and here she was trying to be a good Christian and sharing what she had with him out of the goodness of her heart.

"I suppose you think that's funny," she snapped, and snatched the bread right off his plate, just as he was reaching for it. She slapped it down heavily on the sill with the other loaves, and grabbed up that puny little one instead, and put that on the plate before him—and saw that his bowl was filled almost to over-flowing with her fish stew, and she thought with a surge of anger of how much that cod had cost her at the market, even when she had been able to get Mister Clark to lower his price for her, pleading her new widowhood status.

She would have taken the bowl back once again, even if he was already dipping his spoon into it, but she looked into his face then, and it gave her a start. He no longer looked plaintive at all, or abject. His eyes glinted with an odd kind of light that seemed to stab right through her. And had he had that beard all the time, she didn't remember that, or his hair so long and white? He looked like one of those Biblical prophets, even to the funny robe he was wearing.

"I have heard about you," he said. "The things your husband had to say...." He shook his head.

"My husband? What do you know about my husband?" she demanded, trying to sound indignant, but even to her own ears, her voice sounded more frightened than angry. "Who are you?"

He ignored her question—and for a man who had been starving only a little while before, he now seemed to have precious little interest, she noted, in that bowl spilling over with stew and that enormous, fat loaf of bread before him.

"I wanted to see for myself," he said, "I hoped that it wasn't true, but I can see that it is."

He had a staff in his hand—she didn't remember that either—and he pointed it at her, and banged the end of it on the floor.

Just like that, she vanished.

* * * * * * *

Wilbur was delighted, of course, when the companion he had wished for all along suddenly appeared in the bowl with him.

He quickly realized, however, that he could not call her Orville, and it was not long after that when he recalled something else that the Old Fish had told him: "Be careful what you wish for. You may get it."

He soon learned, though, how to get out of her way. The opening in his castle seemed to have grown smaller, so that he could still pass through it but she, considerably plumper about her middle, could not, and she apparently was nearsighted, because when he hid in the fronds, she could not find him to nip at his fins as she was wont to do.

He found that the best thing to do was to avoid her as much as possible, and stay to himself, and luckily, the bowl was plenty big enough to allow for that.

The good news was, though, that there was a man out there who saw to it that he was fed regularly, and since he was younger and a better swimmer than the newcomer, who just could not seem to get the hang of it, he generally got the best of the flakes.

After a while, the man was replaced by another man and a woman, and a little girl, who liked to make funny faces at him, and he performed for her delightedly, and sometimes she rewarded him with those delicious tiny shrimp that he particularly loved, and he always got the best of them first, and while his bowl-mate was getting what was left, he would retire once again to the little den he had made for himself among the fronds and savored his new found pleasure in solitude.

It was too bad, though, that he could not have had his Orville.

GOOD CHRISTIAN WOMEN, REJOICE

The Marlowe twins, Edna and Eula, were the very models of the "church lady" of modern urban myth. Spinsters of an indeterminate age, they dressed alike in a seemingly inexhaustible stock of dresses in faded pastels—pink and yellow and lilac—all of them with high necks and hems that hovered just inches above their slim ankles.

They might have been pretty once, briefly, in their youth, but their soft-featured faces were doughy now, pale to the point of ghostliness, and devoid of makeup except at Christmas time when they each wore a faint hint of rouge on their lips, and pale flowers painted on their cheeks, long after their season, as if decorating themselves for the holiday. They did not wear their gray hair in buns, as some of the ladies at their church did, but it was cut short in close-fitting curls, and they wore no jewelry except their matching crucifixes.

The Misses Marlowe lived two houses down from me in a little white cottage trimmed in green, with a neat lawn bordered with discreet flowerbeds. From this modest-looking headquarters, the ladies managed their business, which was, as they saw it, to act as the conscience of their community.

I had long since concluded that neither of the ladies possessed an iota of wit and certainly naught of humor, nor indeed any appreciable intelligence, but in its place they had an uncanny instinct for the weaknesses or failings of others. There was no sin, great or small, no fall or misstep from grace, that the

Marlowe twins did not know of it in a trice and make it their business to apprise others of it as well. It was from them that the Duffys down the street learned that their teenage daughter was pregnant, before the daughter herself was entirely sure.

"It was the after school visit from the boyfriend," Edna explained to the parents. She gave the impression that, if necessary, she and her sister could supply the date and the actual moment of impregnation, and any other particulars that might be of interest.

The parents of Timmy Connelly, Hoagie McIntrye, and Ralph Bartlett learned from the Edna and Eula, over glasses of heavily sugared iced tea, that the boys had discovered the joys of masturbation while playing in the tree-house in Timmy's back yard, though not even with the spyglasses they kept to hand by their kitchen windows could those determined ladies conceivably have seen into that leafy retreat.

Distance seemed to deter them no more than foliage. They were able to tell his wife that while Jeremiah Billingstoke was in Minneapolis on his regular buying trip for his hardware store, he had hired a prostitute to come to his hotel room. It is impossible to say how they could have known this. It may be that there exists some secret "Big-Sisterhood," an invisible network of busybodies, who keep tabs on all of us throughout the world and share their information with one another. Or perhaps they possessed some crystal ball, or magic mirror. I do not know. I can only say that their knowledge was utter and uncanny.

No boss flirted with secretary, no married woman checked into a motel at the edge of town during the day, no husband engaged in telephone sex from the privacy of his office, that the Marlowes did not know of it, and report it where it could do the most harm to reputation or standing. This, as they saw it, was their role in life, and they played it with a zeal that would have done the most fervent Reverend Davidson proud.

The house between theirs and mine had been empty for some time; and now it had apparently been sold. The sign came down, and workmen appeared to replace a broken window and make other repairs, and when the painters appeared, the arrival of new neighbors seemed imminent.

The new owners, husband and wife and healthy looking pre-teen son, moved in on a Thursday, and the moving van had scarcely pulled away from the curb outside when Edna and Eula, in faded blue dresses and with little white hats atop their heads, marched with determined cheerfulness up the path and presented themselves at the front door, "To welcome our new neighbors."

I had hoped for an opportunity to give the newcomers some advance warning of what to expect, but I had underestimated the twins' eagerness to investigate their moral standing, and I had been outflanked. I could only watch the door close behind them and wonder what the verdict would be.

I was not long in finding out. Thinking that I was sure to see the Marlowes, if not our neighbors, I dressed for church on Sunday morning, and went a bit early, as Edna and Eula could often be found sharing their latest findings with others in the vestibule.

I was lucky to find them already there and, for a moment, at least, alone. It gave me the opportunity to see how things lay, and I seized it without delay.

"I was hoping I would find our new neighbors here this morning," I said when we had exchanged greetings.

Their smirks were matching. "The Baldanis? I don't think they are the sort for Church services," Edna said coolly, and Eula's head nodded agreement.

"Why ever not?" I asked as innocently as I could manage. "They appeared to be the right sort of people. They dress well, and their furnishings looked quite respectable, and they were certainly polite when I exchanged greetings with them."

They gave one another knowing glances. "We had a most interesting conversation with them on Thursday," Edna said. "I am not one to gossip, as you know, but I can tell you this much: Not only is that man a sinner, but he is quite unrepentant about it. He actually boasted to me of his transgressions."

"That's astonishing," I said. "What on earth did he say?"

"He told me to my very face that he...." But here she quailed, and looked to her sister for support. "I don't think I can say it to a gentleman," she said.

"Oh, but he is not a gentleman, he is a writer," Eula reminded her. "And I believe they are well acquainted with the ways of the flesh."

"Intimately," I murmured my agreement.

"Well, he...." Edna could be seen to summon her courage. "He told me flat out that he is a philatelist. Not only was he quite unashamed to say this, he actually seemed to be proud of the fact. As if that weren't bad enough, the beast had the audacity to ask if we were interested in seeing his accomplishments. Of course, we left immediately. We didn't feel we could linger after that."

"Oh." It took me a moment to grasp the significance of her statement. "Yes," I said after a moment, "he told me of his interests as well."

"You see," Edna said to her sister.

"Quite shameless," Eula agreed.

"I'm afraid there's more," I said in a concerned voice

"More?" The ladies looked utterly nonplussed to think that someone else may have ferreted out sin that had somehow missed their sharp noses. Such a challenge to their supremacy had never before arisen.

"The wife," I said, and looked to and fro, as if fearing that someone had come close enough to overhear, though for the moment no one had. "I learned...." It was my turn to hesitate.

"Of course," Eula said in a burst of inspiration. "You can see right into their kitchen from yours, can't you?"

"Well, only half the kitchen. But I can see their entire back-yard plainly," I said.

"And...?"

"I can't absolutely swear to this—there's all that kitchen I can't see, bear in mind, and who knows what goes on beyond the refrigerator—but I'd be willing to bet money that Mrs.

Baldani is Lebanese."

"I knew it," Edna cried in triumph. "I could just tell."

"The way she looked at you the whole time," Eula said. "I said to myself, there is more here than meets the eye."

"What's more," I added hastily, as the time was nearing for services to begin and by now people were filing into the vestibule, "I am almost certain the son has apnea."

Both ladies clapped hands to their faded cheeks. "Oh, stars," Edna exclaimed. "And he will be starting in to school next week."

"We should warn the principal, I think," Eula said.

"Mister Pittinger?" I said, warming now to my theme. "I'm afraid that might be most *mal à propos*, if you don't mind my saying so."

"But, what can you mean?" Eula asked.

I looked appropriately abashed. "I suppose I shouldn't mention his *avoirdupois*?" I said timorously. "And I believe that he is altogether oleaginous, but I have no doubt you know all about that yourselves, and his cerebration, surely."

"Cere...we had no idea," Edna said, agape.

"In any case, you are surely aware how much of his free time is devoted to horticulture. It quite consumes his evenings, I think."

They gasped in unison. "His poor wife," they cried as one.

"I shouldn't be too worried about her," I said with a wave of my hand "She is a lepidopterist, after all, and a somnambulist to boot. And she was deeply into numismatics, but she assured me she was absolutely cured of that when one of her clients tried to give her a counterfeit silver dollar. She is hardly one to point her finger, I should say."

"Perhaps the Reverend Blessing," Eula said tentatively, by now fanning herself with her missal.

"Perhaps," I agreed. "If only he weren't such a philanthropist. We've talked about it at length."

"Oh, but, he's always seemed so devoted to Mrs. Blessing," Eula exclaimed.

"And I can assure you, he is certainly more homiletic than anyone could ever imagine, just looking at him." I shrugged sadly.

"Poor, dear Mrs. Blessing," Eula attempted to save the day. "She is an artist, you know."

"Dada," I said curtly. "Arp." The ladies were eloquently inarticulate. They stared at me open-mouthed for all the world as if they knew what I was talking about. "Besides, I happen to know...," but here I paused and looked shamefaced. "I don't think...she swore me to secrecy," I mumbled.

"But we are ladies of the church," they cried in one voice. "We have a right."

I sighed. "Phrenology," I said. "She offered once to do it to me."

"Surely you didn't?" Edna said, backing a few inches away from me.

"No, no I could not bring myself to that. I like to think my 'bumps,' as she calls them, are a private matter, and I told her so, but she only laughed gaily, and said she would certainly be in hot water if the church ladies ever learned of her predilection."

"Her...?" Edna said, unable to bring herself even to say the word. But here we were interrupted finally by the arrival of a group of their friends, including Mrs. Blessing, who suggested that it was time to enter the sanctuary.

"I think I shall have to go home," Edna said suddenly. "I am not feeling well."

"Nor am I," Eula agreed, and with no more than the scantest of goodbyes, the twins took themselves hastily out the door and down the steps to the sidewalk.

"How odd," Mrs. Blessing said, looking after them. "I've never known the Marlowe twins to miss a service. I wonder what that was all about?" She turned to me. "But you were engaged in conversation with them. Did they give any clue to what was the matter?"

"I am afraid that for once, words may have failed the ladies,"

I said, and went into the sanctuary, where I took a seat alone in the rearmost pew. I felt that I had much that I must deal with, as I needed both to ask forgiveness for my wrongdoings, and to give thanks for my accomplishments, and it is my experience that prayers of such a discursive nature require considerable concentration.

THE MASTER'S SPELL

AUTHOR'S NOTE: Elliot and Irene have inherited a crumbling château in France, and find themselves visited by a mysterious M. Gastion, who offers to help in the château's restoration, an offer Irene declines because she finds their visitor oddly repulsive.

* * * * * *

> Will you, I pray, demand that demi-devil
> Why he hath thus ensnar'd my soul and body?
> William Shakespeare

> What potions have I drunk of siren tears,
> Distill'd from limbecks foul as hell within.
> William Shakespeare

Irene was in the dining room of the hotel the following morning when the proprietress, a plump, nervous little hen of a woman, came bustling in from her own apartment in the rear.

"Ah, Madame, I am glad to see you," she said, wiping her hands on her apron. She was out of breath, as if she had been hurrying. "I shall not be able to serve you lunch today. I am called away."

Irene was in the habit of having her lunch at the hotel, but the food was no more than mediocre, and she did not much mind having to go elsewhere. "It's quite all right," she said.

After a pause, the proprietress volunteered the information that Irene had not asked for. "It's my mother," she said.

Judging from the tone that something more was expected of her, Irene said, "I hope it's nothing serious."

The woman was altogether pleased at this opportunity to bemoan the fates that treated her so unkindly. She made a gesture of despair and wrung her hands together.

"Life is so hard," she said. "And my mother, ah, if only she were not so difficult. She is eighty, you understand, and she lives at a distance. Not that she isn't welcome here, you understand—all these rooms, we would not be crowded, would we? But no, she wants to stay by herself. And now she is sick, and a neighbor calls me and says she is crying for me, and I must come to her, and my husband is away today, so there is nothing I can do but leave the hotel unattended. Life is a plague, is it not?"

"I am so sorry," Irene said. "If I can help...perhaps I can keep an eye on things here?"

The woman's frown softened a little. "Oh, that is kind, thank you, but I doubt that anyone will come today for a room, and if someone comes for lunch, perhaps you will just tell them we are closed for the day."

"Of course," Irene said, and got up to leave, but the proprietress motioned her to remain.

"Please, I do not mean the room is closed to you," she said. "Make yourself at home, I beg you." She bustled back out again, and Irene seated herself once more at her table, where she had been writing letters to friends back in the states.

Less than an hour later, the proprietress again came through, this time dressed in a street dress and a frayed coat, and carrying a little satchel. They exchanged goodbyes, as if she might be leaving for days, and then Irene was alone in the room once more. For all she knew, she might be alone in the hotel. There had been only one other guest of late, an Englishman who had stopped on his way south, and he had gone yesterday.

She finished her letters and prepared the last of them for

mailing. There was a little restaurant near the post office, and it was not long until lunchtime. She thought she would stroll in that direction and mail her letters, and then have something to eat. Afterward, she would go by the house. Or perhaps not, she thought upon reflection. Eliot would not be pleased to see her, and she would not be pleased, she was certain, to see how the work was going; and she was sure to encounter M. Gastion if she went to the house.

She was quite surprised, then, to see M. Gastion when she stepped to the sidewalk a little later. He was passing slowly by, and as he did not seem to have seen her emerging from the hotel, she deliberately shrank back into its shadows, hoping to avoid a meeting.

Suddenly he came to a stop and clapped one hand over his heart. With a cry, he sank to his knees on the pavement. As Irene watched in horror, he fell flat upon the ground.

He had been stricken ill, and there was nothing that she could do but go to him and see if she could help. She hadn't a hard enough heart to allow her to remain where she was in the doorway and watch the man die. However much she disliked him, no man stood so low as that in her esteem.

Her heart pounded as she went to him. He looked pale, and might even have been dead, except that she saw him open his mouth and gasp for breath. She knelt down, looking around for assistance, but the street, never particularly crowded, was deserted. She was at a loss what to do, when he opened his eyes and saw her.

"Ah, Madame l'Américaine," he gasped, "Help me inside, I beg you, out of this sun."

"But I don't think I can," she stammered, sure that she could never manage to carry him or drag him inside.

"Help me," he begged. He struggled to get to his feet, and with her help he was able to do so. He leaned heavily upon her, but with their combined efforts they managed to get him into the hotel dining room, where he sank weakly into one of the chairs.

"Let me get you some water," she said.

"No—there are some tablets in my left-hand pocket. Get me one of those, please."

She found the pills in a case and gave him one, which he swallowed.

"It's my heart," he whispered. "It does not often trouble me, but when it does, it can be severe. I might have died today had it not been for your kind assistance."

"I'm only grateful I was nearby at the time," she said.

He closed his eyes and although he seemed to be breathing more easily, she saw that he wanted to rest. She moved quietly about the room, restless and yet not wishing to be rude and simply leave him alone. The curtains were open, but a large tree sheltered the windows, so that the room was dim and gloomy, but she could appreciate that in the hot weather it might be cool. On one wall was a cheap print of the *Gioconda*, and in a corner a dilapidated old piano, which had not been played since Irene had been there; and not, she suspected, for a long time before that.

"I am intruding," M. Gastion said from his chair.

She turned to look at him. He looked better now and his voice was steady. She realized for the first time that he had an odd way of looking at a person: when most people look at you, their eyes seemed to converge upon you, but his remained parallel, as it were, so that he seemed to be looking not at but through you, at something beyond.

Meeting his gaze, as intimate as ever, she found her pity leaving her, and again she was filled with dislike for the man.

"Anyone would have done the same," she said indifferently.

He sensed at once the change in her manner, and said, "I think I should leave you now."

He got up from his chair, but he had taken no more than two steps before he groaned and stumbled, and once again went to his knees. She sprang to help him, and as she did so, she felt a wave of guilt at her rudeness to a man who was obviously quite ill.

"I'm sorry," she said, helping him back to the chair in which he had been sitting. "Please, stay as long as you like. Can I get you anything? I'm sure the proprietress will not mind if I bring you some brandy."

"Nothing," he said, dismissing the suggestion with a wave of his hand. "Only let me sit here for a little while."

"As long as you like," she said, standing by him, helpless and conscience stricken. "I'll stay here with you until you are better."

He closed his eyes again, and thinking he would rest, she went to another chair and sat in it, putting one hand to her temples. She felt oddly disturbed by this scene that was taking place. Her heart was beating uncommonly fast, and the room seemed to have become warm and very close, although the day outside was cool.

After a time, he asked, "Can you really dislike me so much?"

Without looking at him, she asked, "What difference can it make, whether I like you or not?"

He gave a great sigh that frightened her because she thought for a moment he was having another attack, but then he spoke again. "If you knew how lonely and unhappy my life has been, you would have a little pity on an old man," he said.

There was something pathetically moving in his voice as he said these words, so that she did indeed feel a wrench of pity in her heart. That he was sincere she had no doubt, and she felt that she had been unnecessarily cold toward the man, for no valid reason.

"You think I am being selfish in butting into your lives," he went on, without waiting for a reply from her. "You will not give me credit for truly wanting to help you. Do you think that I do not long for your approval, for your friendship? But how am I to have it, if you will not let me earn it?"

She sat in silence, listening. There was something different about his voice, something silken and seductive. She did not know why, but its soft, low murmur seemed to make her pulse quicken.

"I disgust you, I know," he said. "I can see it in your eyes when you look at me."

"No," she said, but she knew her denial sounded insincere, as it was. He seemed to read her thoughts.

"It breaks my heart that you feel so toward me. You are good and pure, I can see that, and it makes me feel unclean to think of your dislike for me. I feel that I must be less than human."

She had not meant to look at him and yet against her conscious intention, she did so. She was surprised to see he looked quite different. His eyes had a new expression in them that she had not seen before. They were tender, and glistening with tears, but with some strange invitation, too. His mouth trembled as he returned her gaze.

"You are so beautiful," he said, his voice sinking yet lower. He was speaking now in little more than a whisper, and yet his words seemed to echo in her mind, not so much as if she heard them, but rather as if she felt them within her.

"Beautiful, and a little weary of the world, I saw that when I first laid eyes on you. Yours is not merely an outward beauty, either, but something that glows from within, something that gleams out from secret thoughts and strange dreams and beautiful passions. I look at you and I see all of the world, all the history of man. I see in your eyes what men have seen in the *Mona Lisa*, that knowledge of the secret mysteries of life, and of love."

His voice was soft and musical, and she was intoxicated by the sound of it. She scarcely weighed his words, and yet they stirred something within her, some dark part of her soul that moved restlessly and seemed to awaken slowly from a deep slumber.

"You are older than time, and as young as tomorrow," his voice droned on, unbidden by her. "You have died before, and learned the secrets of death, and lived again. You are Helen of Troy, and Cleopatra, and Saint Anne, and you and I have been together through all history."

He began to speak then of himself, and he spoke openly,

frankly, with no fear of shocking her. Indeed, she was not shocked, although he spoke of things not commonly discussed between a man and a woman who were only casually acquainted. He painted a portrait for her, a portrait of himself, and it quickly began to take form before her eyes, as clearly as if it were painted with oil paints upon canvas or on glass. She saw him as he truly was: cruel and indifferent, indolent and passionate. He was sensual and at the same time, a cold man. In his mind dwelt unnatural knowledge, and crimes for which he bore no guilt, and lusts that belonged more to the lower animals than to man.

Yet for all of that, she saw that he was *man*, a multitude of men throughout the ages of history. He made himself one with an army of spirits that paraded before her, all linked in their evil, in their thirst for dark knowledge. He was all the evil that had ever been. He was every wicked man who had ever lived.

His words seemed to trace a pattern on her soul. She was filled with a strange sense of sin and decadence, and of passion. She wondered what was happening to her, but she was powerless to resist.

She sat in silence, listening. She was disgusted and yet fascinated by what he said. His eyes held hers so that she could not look away, and his voice seemed actually to reflect the very beating of her heart. She had a peculiar languorous feeling. She might almost have been asleep. Her limbs were weightless, and she doubted her ability to move them at all.

He ceased speaking finally, and still she sat silent and motionless, as if she were waiting, although she did not know for what. She heard and saw him rise from his chair and she wondered almost unconcernedly what he was going to do next. She saw that he had recovered completely from his earlier attack, but she made no comment on this.

There was a bowl, a cheap ceramic thing, on the table near where she sat. He took something from his pocket as he came across the room, and he dropped it into the bowl. It seemed to her that he did nothing more than gesture above the bowl with his hands, but suddenly a low flame sprang to life in the bottom of the dish. A thick odor came from it and filled the room. Irene inhaled it and found it pungent and repulsive. She coughed. She wanted to beg him to take it away, but she could not find her voice. She had no control over her physical being. Her body did not obey her.

He lifted the bowl in his two hands and held it toward her. "Look," he said, "look into the bowl."

She did not hesitate, but did as he had commanded, and looked into the dish. The blue fire that had burned within it was not a fire at all. It was something strangely alive, something that writhed eerily, like blue serpents.

"Breathe," he ordered her, and she did as he said. A sudden darkness came down over her, and she trembled violently. She tried to scream, but no sound came from her throat. Her brain reeled and she had a sensation of spinning about, head over heels. She felt suddenly as if she were moving through the air, traveling at a terrible speed, and she was terrified. It was like being caught up in a hurricane.

"Open your eyes," he said finally. Her movement had ended.

She opened her eyes and looked about. It was night, but not the calm restful night she had known often in the past. This was a troublesome darkness, filled with vague whispering sounds, like the passing of giant birds overhead. Lights flickered here and there, like fireflies, and she saw that they stood on a great wasteland of rocks and cliffs and twisted trees. She knew that M. Gastion held her hand, and she was glad for its feel. It was as if she had traveled to the land of every childish nightmare, of every troubled sleep.

At last she saw that they were not alone in this darkness, for the air about them was filled with shadows, forms that swept close and then drifted back, like the waves breaking upon the shore, and came again, closer, closer.

Then, suddenly, all was still, and instead of darkness there was an eerie green light. She saw before them one tree, twisted and wasted. It appeared to have suffered great pain and torment, as if it were human, or more than human. Its tortured branches were lifted like the arms of a giant, in anguish.

She watched, sick with fear, and the tree came to life, the branches became arms, the roots clinging to the earth became feet. But this was no human form. It was brutish and horrible, with horns and a shaggy beard, and hairy legs that ended in hoofs. The face was human and yet not human, grotesque with lust and cruelty, and yet somehow wildly appealing. The lecherous eyes caressed her, and she could almost feel their touch.

The creature shimmered and seemed to melt, and he became altogether a man, a beautiful young man. He was the Michelangelo Adam, the Donatello David. He was Salome's Iokanaan, with the body whiter than "the breast of the moon when she lies on the breast of the sea." He was sublime, naked, and full of majesty, and she wanted to touch him, to sink into the abyss of his eyes. In his smile was all the sorrow of the world, and all the wickedness.

"Do not be afraid," M. Gastion said beside her. "I have an art for which all things are possible. It controls the elements and the stars and the planets. I can make the moon fall blood red from the sky, and the dead rise up and speak with the night wind. Heaven and Hell obey me, and all forms, and all feelings. I am all that is, and has been, and will be. Life and death are in my right and left hands, and immortality is my province."

Before her, the youth beckoned and she felt once more something dark and unknown stir within her.

At last she spoke. In a whisper, she said, "Show me." She did not know for what she asked. Some part of her mind knew that something horrible was upon her, and that part of her beat like an imprisoned bird with helpless flutterings against the cage that held it; but she knew that it was too late now to draw back, that with her words she had somehow sealed a bargain between them.

The youth disappeared into a cloud, and once again a throng of spirits surrounded her. They took form now, and she saw all of the foul beasts and legendary monsters that man had ever fancied. They defied description. They crept and crawled and leapt. They were winged, and slimy, and scaly, and some were nearly human, but they were the condemned of Dante's *Inferno*, and when they laughed it was like the knell of death.

A woman approached her, holding out a chalice of wine. Irene took it, and drank, and it was blood that spilled from the corners of her mouth, staining her blouse.

A sudden fire burned in her veins, and she could almost feel her soul fleeing, and another taking its place. She knew all that was wicked and evil and obscene. Before her eyes a hideous festival of lust was taking place, and she was a part of it. It was indescribably horrible, and yet she responded to it as a violin responds to the bow that plays upon its strings. Beside her, M. Gastion laughed with derision.

* * * * * * *

"You will be all right now," he said, and suddenly his voice was natural, and they were again in the dining room of the little hotel. She looked around, frightened. Everything was as it had been before. There was still that unpleasant odor of the substance he had burned in the bowl.

She remembered her dream then, and remembered that this man before her had been in it, and she was seized with an awful shame. Her cheeks burned and she put her face in her hands and began to cry.

"Please leave me," she sobbed. "Go away."

He smiled, and nodded his head, and without a word left her. She closed her eyes briefly, and when she looked up he was gone, although she had not heard him leave.

A moment later she heard a sound on the street. She was afraid he had come back and she jumped to her feet, prepared to flee from him into the village rather than remain alone with him again; but it was the proprietress who came in, looking flushed and out of breath.

"It's terrible," she panted, banging her satchel down upon a table. "The jokes they play these days, on a woman of my advanced years. An hour's train ride there and an hour's train ride back, and all for a joke."

"Is your mother all right?" Irene asked mechanically, making an effort to regain her composure.

"There was nothing at all wrong with her," the woman said with an angry snort. "It was a practical joke, that was all. Has anyone been in?"

"No, no one." The lie slipped out unbidden. She was surprised to have said it, and her cheeks colored.

The proprietress sniffed the air. "What's that awful smell? Have you had lunch?"

Irene felt an overwhelming urge to be alone. "Yes, I ate out," she said, starting toward the stairs that would take her up to her room.

"You've forgotten your letters," the landlady said after her.

The letters Irene had written earlier were still lying on the table by her handbag, waiting to be posted. It felt a century ago that she had started out to mail them.

She went toward them, but before she reached them, the landlady said, "Oh, you've hurt yourself."

Irene stopped and looked down. To her horror she saw that her blouse was stained with blood, turning now from red to brown. She remembered in a vivid flash of memory the chalice of her hallucination, from which she had drunk wine that had turned to blood. In a flash, she saw that entire scene again, and she gave a little gasp of anguish.

On an impulse she seized the letters she had written and began to tear them to shreds. She threw the scraps into the waste receptacle by the stairs and, without a word to the astonished proprietress, she ran up the stairs to her room.

* * * * * * *

Irene did not mention her visit with M. Gastion when Eliot came later. She had managed very nearly to persuade herself that it had been altogether innocent and that she had let her imagination run away with her. She had been under a strain, after all, and everything was so strange here and foreign to her, it was not surprising that she should have funny dreams.

She decided she would mention quite casually that M. Gastion had been by. "Not," she meant to add quickly, "To pay a visit. He got sick as he was going by outside, and I made him come in and sit here a while." She also intended to remind Eliot that she did not care for the man at all.

When Eliot came in late that afternoon, however, when he kissed her and she saw his simple, trusting love for her in his eyes, she felt embarrassed and oddly guilty. The words she had intended to speak stuck in her throat, and she let the opportunity of speaking them pass by; and after a while, it would have been awkward to bring them up. Eliot would surely wonder why she had not mentioned them at once.

It was Eliot, in fact, who, much later in the evening, brought up the subject. "M. Gastion was by," he said when they were preparing for bed. "He asked again about taking charge of the restoration, and he asked me if I would bring the matter up with you once more. He seemed to think you might have changed your mind. Of course, I told him it was only a waste of time, that when you made your mind up to something, it stayed made up."

Irene was seated at the little dressing table, applying cream to her face. She paused in her ministrations and looked into her own frightened eyes in the mirror. She fancied that it was not her own face there, so pale and drawn, but the face of a stranger, a woman she did not even know. For a moment she thought she saw M. Gastion, standing just behind her in the glass, grinning at her. He reached a hand toward her bare shoulder, and she gave an involuntary shudder, but it was only a phantom of her imagination. No coarse hand touched her satin skin, and when she looked again, there was no one present but Eliot, watching her curiously from the bed.

"Are you all right?" he asked.

"Yes, of course," she said, "why shouldn't I be?" She dabbed furiously at her face with the cream.

"You looked so, I don't know exactly. Stricken, I suppose, is the best word."

"I was...I was thinking of the landlady. She had a terrible practical joke played upon her today. Someone called to say that her mother was sick, and she made a two-hour trip there and back, to discover it was only a prank."

She removed the cream with a towel and put it aside. "Perhaps you've been right about M. Gastion," she said, coming to bed. "M. Bernard seems to be getting no better, and the work has come to a virtual standstill. Perhaps it would be foolish to continue to refuse M. Gastion's offer."

Eliot looked both surprised and relieved. "Yes, that's true," he said. "After all, he may be an agent of divine providence."

She said nothing in reply to that, although she looked at him for a long moment before turning out the light.

They made love, and Eliot was surprised and delighted by the intensity of his wife's ardor.

* * * * * * *

They moved the following day into the house in the country. The rooms that she and Eliot would occupy were in the rear of the second floor, so that she had a view of the woods and the old mill. She did not immediately put herself to unpacking, but went instead to the window seat and stared out at the view. Despite its loveliness, she would have given anything in the world to have it traded for the skyline of Manhattan. She longed to be gone from here, to be home—she considered New York her home, and always would—to have all this undone, as if it had never happened. She felt inexpressibly sad, and tears welled up in her eyes, blurring the scene outside the window and giving it the watery quality of a Monet painting.

She felt so ashamed of herself. It was her nature to be truthful, and she had always been open and frank with Eliot. Several times she had come close to telling him about her visit from

M. Gastion, but something had seemed to impel her, against her nature, to continue to conceal that truth from him, and now she knew she had not the courage to tell him. She could not bear that his trust in her should be destroyed; and if she told him about the visit, she must tell him too about those horrible visions she had had. He would think her insane, as indeed she half feared she might be.

There was a sound at the door, and she gave a terrified cry and leapt to her feet. She thought for an instant that it was M. Gastion, and her eyes were wide with terror as the door opened, but it was her husband.

"Hello, you look a fright," he said, regarding her curiously.

She ran into his arms. She felt physically weak, and for a moment she could only cling to him and give herself up to tears.

Although he was not usually sensitive to feminine emotions, Eliot was a gentle man. He held her tenderly and let her vent her emotions.

At last she sobbed, "Eliot, darling, take me away from here, please."

He laughed softly, thinking then that he understood. His wife was homesick. It was as simple as that. He had observed that she seemed preoccupied, and had been wondering what it was. He was relieved to know it was nothing serious after all.

"Darling, we can't just go away, not in the midst of all this work."

"I want to go home."

"But this is our home," he said, patting her still trembling shoulder. "We gave up everything in New York. It would mean financial disaster for us to try to go back now."

"I have money," she said desperately.

"We've been all through that. Anyway, there's no reason for us to go back. This is our house, the renovations are well under way, and in a few weeks we'll be able to live like a king and a queen here. We can have the sort of life I've always wanted for us."

She listened with diminishing sobs to all that he said. She

knew he would never agree to live on her money, and she could see that he was right as far as the house was concerned. She saw, too, that even if she tried to explain, if she told him what had happened, he would only think she was being foolish.

She freed herself from his embrace and dried her eyes with her handkerchief. Eliot was pleased to see that she had recovered her composure.

"M. Gastion has arrived," he said, thinking to occupy her mind and free it of morbid fancies. "He's going to outline his plans for the rest of the work. Do you want to join us?"

She had been looking down, but now her head jerked up and there was an odd expression in her eyes. It reminded him of the eyes of a deer in a book he had seen as a child. Some creatures not shown in the picture, probably dogs, were after the deer, and the animal's eyes had been filled with the horror of the pursued. The picture had haunted his childish dreams for years. Now, for a second or two, he imagined that Irene's eyes were filled with the same horror.

It was only an instant, though, and then it was gone, and she was cool and collected once more. "No," she said softly. "I think I will take care of unpacking."

"Don't work too hard," he said gently. "We have all the time in the world."

"Have we?" she asked. She did not wait for an answer, but asked, "Has M. Gastion moved into the house, then?"

"Yes. His room is the far east one, on this floor. I forgot, he said to be sure to tell you which it was, in case you wanted him for anything."

She turned her back on him and was silent. Eliot felt uncomfortable, as if there were something he ought to be doing, and could not remember. At length he shrugged and said, "Well, I'll go down to him, then."

He started from the room, but before he had gotten to the hall, she spoke his name. He turned back to her. He could not help but think how lovely she looked, and how strangely vulnerable.

She said, "If anything should happen to me here, the fault will be yours."

He gave his head a shake and smilingly said, "What could happen to you here, of all places? After Manhattan, I should think you'd feel quite safe here. I'll bet there isn't a mugger for two hundred miles."

He had meant to make a joke of whatever was bothering her, but she did not find his remarks amusing. She turned her back on him again and seemed to want him to go.

He hesitated for a moment longer. He remembered that she had been afraid of M. Gastion when they had first met the man; and now M. Gastion had moved into the house with them. He wondered if that could have anything to do with his wife's odd mood.

Yet it was she who had made the decision to have M. Gastion help them, and to let him move into the house. Frankly, he had been more than a little surprised by the decision, although M. Gastion had taken it as a matter of course, as if he had expected this all along—but Irene would surely not have suggested that if she had been still afraid of him.

He shrugged and went out, closing the door gently. He thought, not for the first time, that women were difficult to understand.

* * * * * * *

Irene stayed in her room during the day, and so managed to avoid the sight of M. Gastion. She could not explain this, even to herself. She knew that with him living in the house she must eventually, sooner or later, meet him again; but she could not bear the thought of seeing him, and her thoughts did not go beyond the immediate moment. Her fear was of the present, and tomorrow's fears would have to take care of themselves.

When time came to go out for dinner, as they were not yet set up to do any real cooking in the house, Eliot came up to get her.

"I'm sorry, darling," she said, putting a finger to her temple,

"I have a splitting headache. Do you mind if I just stay here?"

"You aren't coming down with something, are you?" he asked, worried because she really did look a little under the weather.

To his surprise, she only laughed and shook her head, but her laugh was completely without mirth, and a moment later she threw herself across the bed in an attitude of anguish. He went to dinner with M. Gastion, and brought her back a cold supper.

Irene lay for most of the night and listened to her husband's untroubled sleep. She wondered grimly if she would ever sleep so easily again—she who had never, not once in her life, been troubled by insomnia. The truth was, she was afraid to sleep, afraid of what visions might come to her when she had crossed over into that realm of darkness and fantasy.

The next day she felt fatigued and highly wrought. She looked back upon her meeting with M. Gastion and felt that it had been no accident. She felt sure that it was he who had pulled the prank on the hotel proprietress, causing her to be away for some length of time, and she was sure too that his illness had been faked, to elicit her sympathy, so as to put her off her guard, and gain time alone with her.

That he had somehow hypnotized her she was convinced, and she knew that she should be angry about this, but oddly, she no longer was angry. Before, she had felt an inexplicable loathing for him, but this emotion too had vanished. Although it dismayed her, she could not get the man from her thoughts. The things he had said to her, and the nightmarish visions he had inspired in her, seemed almost to have taken possession of her, and to have grown. It was as if some evil seed had been planted within her, and had begun to grow, sending its poisonous roots into every artery and vein.

Nothing that she tried distracted her. If she tried to read, she found herself seeing and hearing not the words in the book, but the words of M. Gastion. If she tried to look at the view from the window, she seemed to see the image of him in the glass. Moment by moment, she felt his presence in the room with her.

She was frightened of the man, and yet her fear was without the physical repulsion she had known toward him in the past. She told herself that she did not want ever to see him again, that she would refuse to come into his presence. At the same time, she felt an almost irresistible desire to go to him wherever he was. She was haunted by the knowledge that he was here, within the same house with her, that his room was but a few yards away.

She struggled against this fascination that he had newly acquired for her, but in her heart she was not entirely certain she wanted to resist. She knew that she wanted to be with him, and yet she was terrified of that knowledge. She felt that to yield to that temptation was somehow to seal her doom.

At last she knew that she must turn to someone for help, and she remembered the abbé. She felt certain that gentle man would not laugh at her imagination; and if he could do nothing else for her, he might at least be able to persuade Eliot that it was best they go away from this place.

She stole from the house without a word to Eliot, afraid that if she went in search of him, she should encounter M. Gastion as well. She chided herself that she was being foolish, but at the same time she had an idea that she must at any cost avoid another meeting with M. Gastion.

It seemed to her that she had not a moment to lose, and she hurried to see the abbé, but, there, she learned that he was out.

"It is the day he goes around to visit the sick," the little sister at the door explained. "They are scattered about. I doubt that he will be back before evening, perhaps not until quite late."

Irene's heart sank. She felt as if her last hope had been taken from her.

The nun, watching the dark expression that spread over the visitor's face, asked, "Would you like to come in and wait? Perhaps he will not be so very late."

Irene hesitated, but she saw that she could not just disappear for the entire day without alarming Eliot. She shook her head and started away without a word.

"Shall I give the father a message?" the worried sister called after her.

Again, Irene hesitated. But what message could she leave for the abbé? And what good would it do? He would not be back until night, and it was now that she needed his help. What did she care about the future, when she could not endure the present? She went on without even a reply to the sister.

When she arrived back at the house, it was to receive yet another disappointment. One of the workmen came to tell her that Eliot was gone.

"He had to go into the city to make some purchases," the man explained, "and he said to tell you that if he was not back before nightfall, not to worry, as M. Gastion would be here, so you wouldn't be alone in the house."

She murmured some word of thanks, and fled to the safety of her room, but there was no comfort for her there. It seemed as if all fate was conspiring against her. She felt helpless to resist the forces that were at work. She was like a drowning person, clinging to a rock. The waves dashed over her, clawing at her, drawing her inexorably into the turbulent waves.

She tried to pray, which she had not done since she was a child, but even the words of her childhood prayers eluded her and refused to come to her tongue.

She prowled her room like a caged animal, counting off the seconds. If only she could endure until Eliot returned home— but each second was an eternity. She paced and suffered, and felt that surely an hour must have passed, only to discover, when she looked at her watch, that it was no more than a few minutes since she had last checked the time.

She locked the door to her room, only to rush back to it a moment later, unlock it, and fling the key through the open window.

At last she could struggle no longer. She threw open the door to her room and went into the hall. The house was silent. The workmen had left, and she knew that she was alone in the house with her tormentor. Despite this fact, she crept along the corridor stealthily, as if afraid she might be seen. Her heart was pounding. With all her might, she tried to resist the urge drawing her along the hall, and yet she went, until she was before the door she knew was his. She stood trembling for a moment.

Finally, she knocked.

(Excerpted from *The Glass Painting*)

PART TWO
THE UNDERGROUND DINER

LETTERS

Mr. James Fadiman
Fadiman Literary Agency
22 Fifth Avenue, Suite 10000
New York City, NY 10010

Dear Jim,

Finally, after what seems years, here is the literary project I told you last fall that I was working on. I have no doubt that it will be something other than what you were expecting, but, honestly, Jim, I just could not do another Robbie Rabbit book, no matter how much Harper and Row were willing to pay. I can no longer look upon an Easter egg without wanting to commit bunnycide. I've had to attach a roller skate to my little fluffy tail to keep it from dragging on the ground. In short, I am simply all hopped out.

However, I know what a fine literary agent you are and I have absolute confidence in your finding exactly the right publisher for *The Underground Diner*, and I am eager to hear your response, and of course I always welcome any input from you.

Warmest Friendship,

Victor

Mr. James Fadiman
Fadiman Literary Agency
22 Fifth Avenue, Suite 10000
New York, NY 10010

Dear James,

I was of course delighted to hear from you so expeditiously, but I feel that I really must remind you of the many years we have been friends, a friendship thus far unspoiled by any vulgar disagreements. I can only suppose that your advice as to what I should do with *The Underground Diner* was meant to be in the nature of a joke, though I must say your sense of humor has changed dramatically from what it used to be. Also, I should point out that this manuscript represents nearly two years out of my life, and while I have never claimed to be any great writer, I cannot help but think that those efforts are worthy of some reward.

I hope that I will receive some less caustic reply from you in the near future.

Sincerely,

Victor J. Banis

Mr. James Fadiman
Fadiman Literary Agency
22 Fifth Avenue, Suite 10000
New York, NY 10010

Dear James,

No, of course I am not pulling your leg. I can't think why you should even suggest that. And in response to your other question, yes, I certainly have been examined recently by my doctor and for your edification I enclose a copy of his report, which as you can see gives me a clean bill of health with the exception of some hemorrhoidal problems, which I think he makes overmuch of. I do, after all, spend my working days sitting at the word processor.

Well, all right, since you bring the point up, yes, there have been occasions in my life when I have questioned my own sanity, but don't we all at some point or another? The reality is, though, that I consider myself mostly as sound of mind; but I assure you, if I should at any time change my opinion on that matter, I shall let you know post-haste.

In the interim, I hope that you are attempting to find a publisher for *The Underground Diner*, which is, after all, what you are in business to do.

Sincerely,

Victor

Mister Bruce Brown
Happy Acres Rest Home
Velvet, New Jersey 20012

Dear Mister Brown,

I am in receipt of your very kind letter, but I am afraid that some error has been made. While Happy Acres sounds like a very fine place indeed, and judging from the brochure which you have so kindly included, it certainly seems to enjoy a lovely location there on the banks of the Jersey River, nevertheless, alas, I do not feel at the present time that I have need of your offer of assistance, nor do I find myself greatly in need of "rest" beyond the usual seven or eight hours which I nightly take. No, I do not presently take any tranquilizers, if you exclude a martini or two.

It is puzzling that the person who gave you my name asked that he remain anonymous, since if I knew who he was I might be better able to explain this confusion. I think, after all, that probably someone just made a mistake, though I suppose it is possible that we are only the victims of what seems to me a particularly distasteful joke.

Yours Truly,

Victor J. Banis

Mr. James Fadiman
Fadiman Literary Agency
22 Fifth Avenue, Suite 10000
New York NY 10010

Dear James,

It does appear to be one of those periods of mysterious oc-currences that sometimes befall us in our lives. For starters, my manuscript for *The Underground Diner* came in today's mail. There was no letter with it, so I cannot even guess at an expla-nation for its having been sent to me instead of some worthy publisher. One supposes that your secretary has just been care-less.

I have remailed it back to you, needless to say, so that you may continue with your efforts at finding a publisher for this opus. In all likelihood, you already have, and your secretary sent it to me instead of the editor you asked her to send it to. That seems the most reasonable explanation.

The other mysterious occurrence was when, just this after-noon, I ran into our old chum, Ray Kohl, at one of his watering holes, and he has apparently recently come back from New York City, and he told me the strangest tale of running into you at a dinner party in the city. He was quite concerned in telling me that, when he mentioned me to you, you strongly denied that you knew anyone by my name, which both puzzles and worries me, James.

Now, as you know, I am not one to pry into another's private life, and especially where questions of one's health are concerned, but I must say that Ray's description of your behavior was alarming indeed. I don't know if you have been to see your physician recently, and of course I do not pretend to any medical expertise, but I feel certain that "deliriums" (which is the very word Ray used, I swear it) are not to be taken likely. And surely, "foaming at the mouth"—and again I am quoting directly—can only be a symptom of something serious indeed.

Now, Jim, I know that we have had our differences, but I think you know that I am your friend, and all of this greatly disturbs me, particularly your loss of memory.

I recently received a brochure from a Mister Bruce Brown of Happy Acres Rest Home in Jersey—never mind how I happened to come by this, which I am not sure I quite understand myself—but my point is, perhaps you should think of getting away from things for a bit, and Happy Acres certainly sounds like a fine place in which to do so.

You don't, by the by, happen to know Mister Brown, do you? His letters suggest that he is a charming individual.

With gravest concern,

Vic

Dr. M. Ogden
The International Institute for Pseudopsychosexual Research
39 Crescent City Drive
New York, NY 10020

Dear Doctor Ogden,

Thank you for your fascinating and very flattering letter, but I must confess to being just a bit mystified by your statement that "an individual you met at a dinner party" gave you my name and suggested you contact me. To be honest, I know almost no one in New York City, with the exception of my literary agent, Mr. James Fadiman, who I know is not in the habit of passing out my name and in fact, according to a recent report, had altogether forgotten it, which, as I say, leaves me puzzled. Nor am I at all familiar with your branch of science, pseudopsychosexual research.

However, I am always happy to do what I can to further the interests of science, and I shall certainly be happy to answer the questions you posed if that will be of any help to you.

I am afraid I can supply only the date and year of my birth, as I do not know the hour (I'm sure you can understand that my memory fails me on that point, ha, ha).

I am also afraid that I am not familiar with the term, auto-manipulation, but making an assumption based on the use of the prefix, auto, I can say that my habits (as you put them) in this vein began when I was sixteen, but I think I have improved some on them since then. We do get better with most things, don't we, with practice?

I wish you the best success with your important sounding work, and if I can be of any further service, do not hesitate to ask.

Sincerely,

Victor J. Banis

PERSONAL ATTENTION:

Mister James Fadiman
Fadiman Literary Agency
22 Fifth Avenue, Suite 10000
New York, NY 10010

Dear James,

I have always made it a policy not to interfere in the workings of another's business, and I write to you now only as an old and, I trust, dear friend, to ask if you are really confident of your secretary? To make a long story short, I once again received *The Underground Diner* in the mail; I can only assume that she has repeated the same mistake that she made before, in mailing it to me instead of to the publisher you intended to get it.

Needless to say, I have dropped it in the mail to you again, and this time addressed it to your personal attention in bold letters to be sure that it actually landed on your desk, which should presumably guarantee that this won't happen a third time.

Bear in mind, James, that postage is expensive, and I am only a struggling artist who has already made a considerable investment in this particular project.

Victor

Dr. M. Ogden
The International Institute for Pseudopsychosexual Research
39 Crescent City Drive
New York, NY 10020

Dear Doctor Ogden,

What a pleasant surprise it was to hear from you once again, and I am glad to hear that you found my letter so "interesting," though it seemed to me rather a mundane sort of communication.

No, regretfully, I cannot be any more specific about the hour of my birth. I did take your suggest and ask my mother, whose reply was that she had spent quite a few years trying to forget that incident (which I believe is meant to imply that it was a difficult birth) and does not care to be reminded of it. However, she is advanced in years, and her health is not all that it should be, so I did not choose to make an issue of the matter.

As to the subject of automanipulation, no, that was not a typographical error. I truly did not start until age sixteen. Indeed, I was surprised that you said most boys start at age twelve, and some as early as age nine. Frankly, I find difficult to imagine a boy of age nine fooling around in a car, and I wonder that at such a tender age one would even be big enough to see what was coming, or for that matter to reach all those important knobs and controls. I know when I was nine I could barely manage the radio, but I was a bit undersized so my reach was on the short side, certainly in relation to my desires.

And even if I could have gotten it going and managed a straight stretch with it, I certainly wouldn't have been able to get that enormous thing of my father's around a serious bend. Of course, some boys do get their growth early, which must account for the difference, but my parents would not let me even think about beginning until I was sixteen, though of course I tried once or twice to convince them that I was ready before then, which I think is probably typical of most boys, since they are usually eager to get started, don't you agree?

Sincerely,

Victor J. Banis

Dear James,

Just a quick note to tell you I got your priority overnight letter, informing me that you do not have a secretary. I feel guilty, I must confess, about causing the poor creature to lose her job, but the more sensible part of me knows that she was certainly detrimental to the success of your business.

Any word yet on *The Underground Diner*?

Victor

Attn: Mr. Bruce Brown
Happy Acres Rest Home
Velvet, New Jersey 20012

Dear Mister Brown,

I was nice to hear from you again, though I must confess I am no less puzzled than before, as I still do not feel that I need to pay a visit to Happy Acres Rest Home, though I am sure it is a most pleasant facility.

I do assure you, however, if I should at some future time change my mind, and feel the need of your services, I will certainly take your advice and register myself voluntarily. I entirely agree with your statement that to do so would be far more congenial than to find myself there as a result of a court action, though I know of no reason why my family should be contemplating such an action. Are you suggesting that they have contacted you? Or did your anonymous friend mention them? Just curious.

Sincerely,

Victor J. Banis

Dr. M. Ogden
The International Institute for Pseudopsychosexual Research
39 Crescent City Drive
New York, NY 10020

Dear Doctor Ogden,

Well, I am sorry if my information confused you in any way, though I am sure I do not see how. Yes, I am quite sure of the age I quoted in my last letter. As for your puzzlement over these "activities" taking place in a motor car, I should have thought that was the logical place and the one where most boys began, though I know that some are partial to SUVs and large trucks, and of course there are motorcycles and busses that must enter into the experiences of some, though, frankly, busses never interested me, perhaps because I was afraid of having the responsibility for so many different people all at the same time.

As a boy, however, I was fascinated by the possibility of having a go in a big Semi, as I suppose most boys are in the ordinary course of things, and for that reason as a young man I spent a great deal of time hanging out in the huge parking lot at the local truck stop, hoping to catch the eye of one of those truckers who might let me have a go at it, as I was told many of them are genuinely fond of what they do and are more than willing to share the pleasure with young lads, but, alas, the right opportunity never presented itself, so I never did experience that particular thrill. To reiterate, however, yes, for me, it was always in a car.

I cannot quite fathom why you should be so excited over my remarks about my father and about size, but of course I am ignorant of your particular field of study. Yes, absolutely, my father's was the first for me. Is that unusual? I think the same was mostly true with my friends, though I did have one friend whose mother was single, so of course he started with hers.

To clarify, since you ask for a more detailed description, it was white, though for a time there was a black one, which belonged to a friend of the family who was generous in letting me take advantage of it whenever I felt the need. It seemed pretty enormous to me at the time, I thought it was surely the longest one I had ever seen, but that was probably just seeing it through the eyes of an inexperienced young man. I've certainly handled bigger in my lifetime since then, though how it handles and rides has always seemed more important to me than size, and of course if it can move really fast that can be exciting, especially when there is a lot of traffic to compete with and one wants to whip it in and out in a hurry.

Just to be sure I was providing you with the correct information, I have spent some time recollecting these matters. I did look for any old photographs, but my father was not much of a one for keeping pictorial records of that sort of thing, though he did record most of our important family events. However, my memories only confirm what I said before, that until the age of sixteen, and, considering what my father possessed at that time, I would not, when seated, have been able to see where I was going with it, and as big as it was, and especially, as I said, so long, I certainly could not have guided it around a corner, so you can see I would have been a threat to others, though my father handled it beautifully, especially in light of the fact that he really was a smallish man, and I always admired his expertise with it.

Well, I truly hope you find this additional information of use.

Sincerely,

Victor J. Banis

Dr. M. Ogden
The International Institute for Pseudopsychosexual Research
39 Crescent City Drive
New York, NY 10020

Dear Doctor Ogden,

I received your overnight priority mail this morning, and since this seems to be an issue of some importance to you, I will reply in kind and see that this goes out today; alas, however, I am afraid my reply will be a disappointment. Yes, absolutely, my earliest experiences were with my father, who was quite good at it. I just imagined that this was the case for most young men. I am truly grateful that he took so much interest in my needs and wants. I know that a lot of fathers today are too busy with their own interests and pleasures to appreciate what a special sharing this can be between a boy and his father, but mine was ever mindful of those important milestones in a boy's life.

I take pride in knowing that you would find my father "invaluable to the cause of your research and the interests of science," but the sad fact is, he died several years ago in Tucson, where he continued his automanipulation right up to his very last day, and so proved of great assistance to any number of his neighbors in his retirement community; the elderly ladies who were in residence, of course, but a great many of the gentlemen as well. You would be surprised, I believe, to know how many of them came to him for their needs in this vein, and he was equally generous with both sexes. Many of them spoke to me after his passing of their pleasant memories of these hours they spent with him, their visits to the mall, and even just passing the time on some old country road. There was a spot near where they lived with a little mesa and a view of the desert, and that was a favorite location for many.

I must say, this was typical of the old darling. Throughout his entire life, others were always fond of him, and fascinated by him, and he was a great entertainer. There were often visitors to our home, and of course he was ever the center of everyone's attention. He liked to amuse our guests by performing a variety of tricks that he had mastered, some of them quite astonishing, and always to enthusiastic applause when he was finished. I only regret that he never tried to pursue a performing career, with his special gifts, as I am sure that he would have been a great success on the stage, or even in films of the right sort.

I am sending you my mother's address, because I know she would be pleased with your interest in him. She loved him dearly for his special attributes and was always proud of him, and I am sure she will be delighted to tell you anything you want to know about him.

V. Banis

Mr. James Fadiman
Fadiman Literary Agency
22 Fifth Avenue, Suite 10000
New York NY 10010

Dear James,

I really cannot comprehend what is going on with you these days. I just got that damned manuscript in the mail again. Oh, don't worry, I will get it back to you immediately, but I am starting to fear that you have some very sick sort of person around your place who is playing practical jokes on us.

Fortunately, for the sake of our friendship, I could see that the handwriting on the package was not yours. It was far too shaky looking. It appears to have been addressed by some crazy person, or someone who is not far away from that state, at least. Please, Jim, do be very careful, as some nutcase may have his eyes on you.

Victor

Dear Mother,

How delightful to have a letter from you waiting for me when I came home today. I have been meaning to write, but I must say, it does sound as if you're getting plenty of mail these days anyway.

I wish I could offer you some explanation for that letter from Mister Brown at the Happy Acres Rest Home. He has been writing me too, and I am just as puzzled as you are. Frankly, I was half afraid that you had written to them about me. But, no, I assure you, I had not made any plans to have myself committed, and don't foresee any such action in the future, but I swear to you, if I feel myself "losing it," as you put it, I will spare you the disgrace of taking legal action. I really have never wanted to cause you all that embarrassment, but I am afraid I can do nothing about any remarks that your minister should make, and I don't know how he could know anything about my personal life anyway, other than what may have come to him in the form of vicious rumors, and I don't think it behooves a man of God to take stock in that sort of slander, do you?

As for Doctor Ogden, all that I that I really know about him is that he is a man of science and quite pleasant, and he has certainly been interested in my driving skills, which seems a bit esoteric to me, but I am not of a scientific bent, as you know. To be perfectly frank, I have begun to suspect that he is just a bit eccentric, but scientists often are, I think.

As to the question of whether you should or should not share with him the personal details of your marriage to Father, I prefer not to advise you on that matter, as it is one you really should decide for yourself. I was surprised, however, to learn that you had nude photos of him, though I suppose all things considered, I could hardly have expected you to share those with me. As to whether you share them with Doctor Ogden, I'm afraid that too I must leave up to your judgment. How does he look in them, by the way? Just curious.

Oh, dear, I hear the postman at the door, and I am waiting for word on my latest writing effort, so I must dash, and will write you again soon. Let me know if you hear further from Mister Brown. If he becomes a pest, I will have to get firm with him.

All my love, your son,

Victor

Mr. G. Dickson
Fadiman Literary Agency
22 Fifth Avenue, Suite 10000
New York NY 10010

Dear Mister Dickson,

Thank you for your letter of the Fifth, informing me that you have taken over the operation of the Fadiman Literary Agency for the immediate future in place of our mutual friend, James Fadiman. I was certainly shocked and saddened to read about his mental breakdown, but by the merest coincidence, it turns out that I have indeed heard of Happy Acres Rest Home, and have even been in correspondence with their Director, a Mister Bruce Brown, and from all indications it is a fine institution, and I have every faith that they will have James restored to his old, delightful self in no time at all.

Of course, I look forward to working together with you, as I am sure you are a fine literary agent or Jim would never have placed his trust in you.

As to my manuscript, *The Underground Diner*, it is certainly a mystery to me that you cannot find it there in the office, though you have a record of its having been received. There is an explanation as to why his files show it received so many different times, and I will get to that in due time.

I am afraid I must say that Jim's mental state had deteriorated badly in the last few weeks, and Heaven alone knows what he may have done with the manuscript when he wasn't busy dropping it in the mail to me; but I will print out another copy and send it off to you at once, and will be glad to have your reaction to it.

Yours truly,

Victor J. Banis

Attn: Ms. Agnes Feverfew
Happy Acres Rest Home
Velvet, New Jersey 20012

Dear Ms. Feverfew,

I received your letter today and I wish to tell you how sorry I am to hear about Mister Brown. I do not actually know your employer, which is to say, I never had the pleasure of meeting him, but we have corresponded with one another and he was always an intelligent and considerate man.

It is an odd coincidence, wouldn't you say, his suffering a nervous breakdown while treating my friend, James Fadiman, who is a guest at your establishment. Your suggestion is an intriguing one, that something may have come up during their interviews that caused Mister Brown's problems, but I don't think that I can be of much help to you on that score, as, frankly, I have been in the dark all along so far as the cause of James' problems, which brought him to Happy Acres in the first place.

No, I cannot imagine why Mister Brown would be repeating my name endlessly, which I found particularly puzzling; but as I say, we did have some correspondence, and perhaps in the dark recesses of what I can see now must have always been a troubled mind, there is some little item that he intended to discuss with me and never got around to; but I simply cannot imagine what that might have been.

If I think of anything, however, be assured that I will pass it on to you.

Yours truly,

Victor J. Banis

Dearest Mother,

I don't wish to make a mountain out of what is all too clearly a molehill, but I have to tell you, Mom, that I was deeply wounded by your remarks. I cannot even dream why you think you should have had me committed when Mister Brown first suggested it to you—and if you will recall, I was convinced then, and still am, that some horrendous mistake had been made.

I don't know how you got the idea that I have been trading in "filthy stories," as you put it, about my father, but I can assure you that nothing could be further from the truth. In the first place, I have never had anything but the utmost respect for Dad, and in the second, I have not discussed him at all with anyone of late other than Doctor Ogden, and you know all about that, and certainly everything that I told him was flattering, to say the least.

I hope that you will soon be over whatever it was that upset you so, and that when I hear from you again it will be on a more cordial note.

Your son,

Victor

Dr. M. Ogden
The International Institute for Pseudopsychosexual Research
39 Crescent City Drive
New York, NY 10020

Dear Doctor Ogden,

My dear, departed father seems to be a subject of some controversy these days. I regret that your communication with my mother was so disappointing, but I think I should explain that she has been upset of late. She seems to think that I have been saying naughty things about my father, though for the life of me I cannot imagine where she got such an idea. As you are certainly yourself aware, I never speak of him but fondly and respectfully.

I would not be too concerned, if I were you, about her statement that his "equipment," as you like to call it, was nothing special. Let us be frank, Doctor, man to man: women simply do not have the kind of appreciation of that sort of equipment that men do.

I know that my father loved mother very much, but he used to joke about her ineptness with it. He was very proud of what he had, and it was with me or one or two of his closest male friends that he really enjoyed sharing it.

He was always particular about who got a ride and who didn't, and especially about who he let handle it. So, if mother said that it was not at all large, I think you can chalk that up to a "woman's perspective." I assure you, it was not small.

No, unfortunately, as I think I told you before, I don't have any old photographs I can share with you, and it's been so long ago I can't even recall what it was called. But there is no question that it was large. At the time it seemed to me like it was a block long and just about as wide, but more reasonably I think its length and width (or thickness, if you want to put it that way) was more like twenty by four. I think you will agree with me when I say that is pretty large, even by today's standards.

I just got a new one myself, a beautiful green color, and I can assure you it is nothing like that in size. Of course, things were different in the old days, no one thought about environmental damage back then, or what kind of energy it took to operate it, you just drove the hell out of it and consequences be damned.

As usual, I hope that I have been helpful and that your research is going well.

Yours truly,

Victor J. Banis

Dr. M. Ogden
The International Institute for Pseudopsychosexual Research
39 Crescent City Drive
New York, NY 10020

Dear Doctor Ogden,

It was a pleasant surprise to hear from you so quickly, though some of your questions and comments really do strike me as odd; but I confess, I have never been of a scientific bent.

No, to answer your questions, I have never regretted my relationship with my father though I suppose, as you say, it might have been regarded as unique. I truly believe that if all young boys had grown up having the same kind of relationship with their fathers as I did, or at least with some older male member of their families, as I can understand that an uncle or even a big brother could have taught me the same things, the world would be a better place for it.

Yes, I did say that my recent purchase was green, a nice Kelly green, and I cannot fathom why anyone should consider that objectionable, as when I am rambling about I often see others in the same or similar colors.

As to how I was able to come by it, there is really nothing mysterious about that. There is a showroom near where I live, and I had been unhappy with my old one for some time, so I just dropped by one day. The entire operation was accomplished in no time and I left with it the same morning. I had not gone three blocks down the street, I might say, before I noticed two young lads admiring it and talking about it, which of course was most flattering.

Scientifically yours,

Victor J. Banis

Dear Mother,

May I offer you my heartiest congratulations. I have to admit, it came as a great surprise to me, but you have nothing but my very best wishes that you and Doctor Ogden will be happy together. I know that I have described him as perhaps a bit eccentric, but scientists often are, don't you think, and certainly he has always struck me as an amiable man.

Forgive me for saying this, mother, but you have always been a bit too inclined to fret. Just because the good Doctor said he felt he had to marry you in the interests of science does not mean he is not genuinely fond of you. You know how men of science are. In some strange way, it was probably meant as a compliment to you, and I think that is how you should consider it. As to his curiosity about father, well, that is only natural, isn't it? I expect that as time passes he will lose interest in your past.

It was very kind of him to invite me to come live with you, but I think I will have to pass on that. Anyway, despite what he says, I don't see how I could contribute to his research.

As to his statement that he would very much like to have a photograph of the purchase "we discussed in recent letters," I had a friend take some photos yesterday, and as soon as I have the prints back, I will send them. We took some in the garage and some in the driveway and, for the heck of it, we managed to get a couple of shots in traffic, though it did cause some consternation on the part of the other drivers, I can tell you that.

Again, my best wishes to both of you.

Your son,

Victor

Mr. G. Dickson
Fadiman Literary Agency
22 Fifth Avenue, Suite 10000
New York NY 10010

Dear Mister Dickson,

The strangest thing has occurred, which has given me quite a sense of *déjà-vu*. I received, in today's mail....

THE WALTONSBERG WEST PANHANDLE EXPRESS

To our readers:

Starting today, the *Waltonsberg West Panhandle Express* is happy to announce a new weekly column, to appear in our newspaper each Friday morning: to wit, "The Underground Diner," dealing with food and restaurants here in the beautiful Blue Ridge Mountains. So that he can experience these adventures like everyone else, the author of this weekly adventure into fine eating has chosen to eat underground, and so shall remain nameless, but you may be assured, dear readers, that in real life he is well respected locally for his culinary expertise.

Apart from cooking regularly for friends and family, he has contributed more than twelve recipes to various local church and community cookbooks, and was a runner-up in last year's Chili Cook-Off, and a white ribbon winner at the Potomac County Fair three years ago for his Green Tomato Dessert Topping. In addition, he regularly writes the newspaper ad text for both Wal Mart and Food Giant grocery chains, and has created numerous flyers that have been distributed throughout our community, many of them food related.

It is our sincere hope that these valuable and entertaining columns will tempt our readers to venture out to these stellar establishments of which he pens, whose paid advertisements in these pages help us to continue delivering your community newspaper to your doorstep each and every day, for your personal edification.

The Publishers

The Underground Diner
Column for Friday, June 3
A Pancake Repast to Remember

Being that this is his first column for this newspaper, the "Underground Diner," aka yours truly, has decided to break with the usual routine, and instead of visiting one of our delicious restaurants in the area, the Diner and His Friend made a decision to attend the Waltonsberg High School Women's Club's Pancake and Waffle Supper, which has the added allure of being a benefit for the scholarship fund for the Mountain Valley Academy of Tap and Baton. As Women's Club President, Mrs. Marybeth Overjohn, put it so succinctly to us, "Our motto is, 'To put a little fun in your life, try twirling'."

So, last Sunday, The Friend and I backed the Jimmy out of the garage and wended our way to Waltonsberg High School, which is The Diner's Alma Mater, although The Friend went elsewhere, where the pancake and waffle supper is held every Sunday of this month. The meals are served *al fresco* in the high school gymnasium, beautifully decorated with plastic lilies and carnations, and balloons in a rainbow of colors hanging from the ceiling, which lent a festive air to all.

We were seated immediately by a welcoming Vanda Pomeroy, who led us to a pleasant little table for two next to the boy's locker room, the scent of which brought back to The Diner happy memories of the many hours he had wiled away in this very spot as a little niblet. The Friend was initially a trifle disappointed, as she had asked for a window table when we made our reservations, but we agreed once we were seated that, as the windows were located so high up in the wall, they would not have provided us with a view, and in any case, as Vanda pointed out, "There is nothing to see out there but the school busses, and they haven't even been hosed down yet for the week."

We were immediately titillated with the insouciance of the red and white checked paper tablecloths and napkins with matching paper plates and cups, which provided the gymnasium the *mise-en-scène* of an elegant country bistro somewhere in Tuscany.

We were presented with menus immediately upon being seated. The menus had been artistically decorated by Walter Joe Messner, a nineteen-year-old freshman at Waltonsberg High School, with delightful drawings of teensy elves happily cavorting with one another across the upper border in an unidentified little elvin culinary location, some of them in poses that might have raised an eyebrow if The Diner were of the eyebrow-raising ilk, which, of course, he is not, while blithely flipping pancakes and waffles in the air; and in the lower left hand corner a moving sketch of a tearful Mother Hen surrendering her basket of eggs to a band of rapacious and hungry-looking elves bearing skillets and wire whisks; these provided a dramatic element entirely in keeping with the Memorial Day weekend, as it reminded us of the sacrifices of others.

The menu listed more than forty-three different dining options, though our waitress, Gloria Petrelli, informed us that only about a dozen of them were actually on tap on the evening we supped there.

"The menus were printed weeks ago," she explained, "and it would have been just plain wasteful to throw them all in the garbage," which The Diner agreed with the sentiment of, though he had already wasting a considerable amount of time contemplating viands which as it turned out were not going to be available for his partaking of.

Choosing from among the internationally slanted entrées remaining was plenty difficult enough, however. While we ruminated, Gloria brought us our refreshments: iced tea for The Friend ("It's the bottled kind," Gloria explained to us, "because, frankly, I wouldn't trust the water here even if it was boiled to high heaven; I've had a look at those faucets," which we were grateful for her advice) and for me, the house specialty, a buttermilk and lime sherbet "martini" on the rocks, cleverly garnished with a sprig of lilies of the valley (though The Diner was warned against eating the garnish, which might have been sprayed while in the garden, maybe even by the dogs, Gloria could not say for sure, but better to be safe than sorry, as we both agreed, which she reminded me of those faucets).

I waffled, if I may be permitted a play on words, between the Chicken Salad on Sour Cream Pancakes and the Chorizo Waffles with Fresh Tomato Salsa, but I settled finally on what proved to be the *pièce de résistance*, Hog Heaven, a clever twist on the tired old pigs-in-a-blanket that you practically trip over in restaurants these days: pickled pigs' feet wrapped in horse-radish-flavored pancakes, topped with sauerkraut.

The Friend meditated on the Pepsi Peanuts and Cheese Waffles, which sounded like nothing we had ever occasioned before. Gloria explained that these were flavored with Pepsi in the batter and topped with crumbled cheese and peanut butter crackers, the kind they sell in the vending machines at the truck stop; but though she confessed to being sorely tempted, The Friend ultimately chose The Texas Chili Pancakes for her delectation, which were cheddar and cornbread pancakes with a topping of Texas chili (and also, Gloria mentioned that the cheese and peanut butter crackers had been sitting out unwrapped the whole evening, and she was sure she had seen one of them moving, which occasioned The Diner to mention that he had seen some things moving kind of funny out at the truck stop, too, of which he has not made remark at the time, as truck drivers can be hot-tempered).

All of the pancakes and waffles came with a choice of maple syrup or blueberry syrup, which were cleverly served in those Kool Aid pitchers with the smiley face on the side, blue for the blueberry syrup, and pink for the maple ("we tried to find a brown one, but there wasn't a one to be had in that color," Gloria informed us), except, when she was filling the pitchers, Monica Elders got them mixed up, so the maple ended up in the blue one, and the diners kept calling Zoe Pickerwell back to their tables to tell her that they wanted the maple syrup and not the blueberry, and she had to explain to them that that was what they had gotten notwithstanding the color of the Kool Aid pitcher.

With her very first bite of her Texas Chili Pancakes, The Friend rolled her eyes upward and cried aloud in a stentorian voice, "Oh, my Heavens," which the Diner originally interpreted to mean it was delicious, but when she quickly drained her water glass and the Diner's as well, while enthusiastically fanning her mouth, he suspected something was amiss and summoned Gloria, who was there in a trice.

It turned out that Lita Jane Jensen, our *chef de cuisine*, had misread her recipe and added ¼ cup of chili powder instead of the ¼ teaspoon that was called for; but the mistake was quickly rectified and the incendiary culprit whisked away, and Gloria brought The Friend instead a dish of cottage cheese, which she said would ease the burn; and we were also informed that the carton hadn't been opened until this very minute, as she had opened it herself for this emergency, so there was no danger of anything getting into it beforehand, unlike a few of the other dishes in that kitchen, as she expressed it; and The Friend did agree after a while that it had helped, so all was well that ended well on that score.

All entrées come with your choice of home fries, grits, or macaroni salad. I made my choice for the home fries, which were exactly the way I like them, crisp and dripping with bacon grease, but the paper plate had soaked up too much of the grease, in my humble opinion, a problem that The Diner informed Lita Jane Jenson ought to be amended before future suppers were accomplished.

Also ordered were the grits by The Friend, which she kept when her pancakes were removed, Gloria being dead-set against it, but she finally gave The Friend her way, and which she was able to eat if she went slow; and she opined that the lumps gave them an interesting texture and provided a welcome contrast to the rather bland cottage cheese, which in my opinion needs all the help it can get, though of course, cottage cheese was not what The Friend would have ordered except for Lita Jane's mistake; and it wasn't until later that Gloria offered her opinion on those lumps in the grits, but they were eaten by that time, and there is no point in crying over spilt milk, as The Diner always says, though The Friend was less sanguine; and if you have never tried it, it can be off-putting to savor your Hog Heaven with someone gagging at you across the table, although The Diner managed, he is happy to inform everyone.

While we dined, the guests were treated to a veritable festival of entertainment as well. With the room lights dimmed, Laci Coleman, a senior at Walton High School and an honor student at the Mountain Valley Academy of Tap and Baton, tapped and twirled a twinkle light baton to a medley of Ravel's "Flight of the Bumblebee" and "These Boots Were Made for Walking", and it was a very impressive performance indeed, and brought the house down, despite one minor glitch when she tossed her baton clear up into the rafters at the same unfortunate moment that Zoe Pickerwell came through with an armload of pancake orders; but no one blamed Laci for that mishap, which everybody agreed could happen to just anybody, and she got a standing ovation irregardless.

Once the crockery and the pancakes had been cleaned up, Marsha Cole (who is eighty-seven and no relation to Laci) demonstrated the One-Person-Waltz for us, which, as she explained, provides an excellent limbering up exercise for seniors, which I for one will want to remember in a few years' time, while at the same time allowing you to savor your Lawrence Welk records (though Marsha did warn about debarking on a polka without proper warm-up) and requires no partners or special equipment. You can even, as she pointed out, if you don't have a hi-fi, just hum to yourself while you dance, which is what she did, as the music equipment had suffered some damage from Zoe Pickerwell's accident and a direct hit from the baton and now would not function. I think everyone enjoyed the demonstration anyhow, and it was generally agreed that Marsha is a fine hummer and surely the best one-person-waltzer we had ever seen, though The Diner had hoped for a polka before she finished, as he was curious as to how she would manage that with her walker.

The Diner knew from the minute he saw it on the menu that he would have to try the House Special Dessert: a Slow Gin Fizz Meringue Pie, which Gloria declared firmly did not actually contain any gin, inasmuch as the school does not have a liquor license and she could be arrested for serving it if it did and she did not care to spend Sunday night with Sheriff Abernathy, in or out of that filthy jail of his, whom she described as a foul-breathed moron; but she laughed when she said it to show that it was only a joke. Try though we might to tempt her, however, she refused to divulge the secret of the recipe for the pie, which was made at her home and carried in, so she knew exactly what was in it and what was not, as she enunciated, and which did indeed taste as if it had been liberally laced with gin—Beefeaters, The Diner would have sworn, though he is no expert, as his expertise is limited. He can only say that by the time he had finished licking his plate (just kidding, ha, ha), The Diner was so stuffed that his words were coming out slurred as sometimes happens to him when he encounters an abundance of well prepared and hearty examples of the *arts culinaire*.

The Friend, who had eaten all of her cottage cheese and grits and had finished with her gagging, helped herself to a portion of The Diner's pig's trotters (because, as she explained when he caviled about this, the gelatin was cooling to her mouth) while he was watching the entertainment, settled for a plateful of cookies, which were cleverly baked in the shapes of batons and what The Diner initially thought were little canoes, but which it turned out were meant to represent tap shoes. (Huzzas to Roberta Farnsworth for her artistry in the oven, in passing.) The

Friend declared that they were tasty, too, though she preferred them dipped in her coffee to soften them a little, as her mouth was still sore despite the pig's trotters. The Diner tried one and agreed with her that they were tasty but a little too hard for his liking, and decided on another slice of the Slow Gin Fizz Meringue Pie, the consumption of which cast a warm and merry glow indeed over the rest of the evening, though The Diner was so sated by now that he found himself in danger of nodding off a time or two, which The Friend teased him about when he made some snoring noises strictly as a joke, which fooled her, as he is a born actor.

A nearly perfect evening was marred, however, by one unpleasant incident, which occurred while we were savoring those delicious codas to our meal. It seems that Audrey Mason, who had volunteered as dishwasher, had brought her little Schnauzer with her, whom she has named Gourmet in honor of someone we all know (though she pronounces it "Gour-may," which she says is French and she thinks is more elegant, but I am quite contented with the good-ole American pronunciation, and I can't imagine anyway why a German dog should need a French name, but, of course, The Diner's proper concern was pancakes and not dog's monikers, as Audrey was at pains to point out when he questioned her on this *contretemps*).

The reason Audrey had brought little Gour-may with her is that she is nervous about going out alone and always carries a police whistle around her neck and a can of pepper spray in her pocket, since the incident three years ago when someone stole her newspaper off her porch. "That intruder was within inches of my front door," she points out in every conversation, regardless of the subject matter on which it started out. Also, she keeps a ladder at her bedroom window and the window open at all times, summer or winter, with a bucket and a snow shovel at hand in the winter for the driftings, and she sleeps with all her clothes on because, as she explains, aside from the fact that it is cold in the winter with the window open, but more importantly, if she had to make an escape from an intruder, she would not want to descend the ladder in her nightgown, as she would be screaming for help the entire time, and she is fearful that old Mister Cooper from next door, whom she suspects of peeking in her windows at night anyway, might arrive before she reached the bottom of the ladder, and she wouldn't trust him not to look up.

Well, it seems that Audrey got all caught up with her dishwashing, and as the showers were still running and she already had the rain slicker on, she decided to give little Gour-may a shampoo, which saved her having to do it when she got home later, as this is a regular Sunday event at her dwelling.

When she came back from the showers, she waited while Zoe Pickerwell picked up her orders (which was a slow process because of what had happened to her wrist earlier) from the card table where Lita Jane Jenson placed them as the dishes were gotten ready (the gymnasium not having an actual kitchen, this was all set up in the locker room, which added to the aromas wafting around our heads. "We could have used the cafeteria," Lita Jane explained to us later, "But this is all about money and we felt we could seat more people in the gym, and anyhow, pancakes don't require much in the way of cooking equipment"); and as some dirty dishes had been left while she was away, Audrey took them to the showers, and she left little Gour-may sitting on the card table to be dried when she got back, and she admits that she saw Gloria place the dish containing The Friend's returning Texas Chili Pancakes on the table, but she just thought nothing of it because, as she said, "You couldn't pay that dog to eat a pancake, but I never gave a thought to that there chili."

Well, to make a long story short, Gour-may wasn't satisfied till he had helped himself to that chili, and he got nearly all of it down before the reality of it hit him, and he was so incensed by it that he leaped straight up in the air, "Like a rocket taking off at Cape Canaveral," as Lita Jane described it, and on his first bounce, he went straight for her, and she was so startled to be set upon by a wet dog with his tongue lolling out, whom she was fearful had just been stricken with rabies, not yet knowing about the chili, that she tried to fend him off with her pancake flipper, and instead knocked over the Propane camp stove into the skillet with the bacon grease, and started a fire.

Vanda Pomeroy heard the stove go over and came to investigate, and when she saw the fire, she rushed to the showers to try to get Audrey's rain slicker off of her, which was intended for use by all, to put the flames out, but with all the dog shampooing and dishwashing, there was so much steam in the shower room that Audrey couldn't see a thing and was only washing the dishes by touch, and Vanda had to grope blindly for the slicker, and Audrey thought she had been set upon by some errant basketball players.

"It is the boy's locker room, after all," as she pointed out in her own defense. "We would have used the girls, but it happens there was a toilet stopped up and Lita Jane said she couldn't cook in there as so much of what she does she uses her nose, so we had to move everything over to the boys, and I was worrying all evening what would happen if some of them needed to take a shower."

Well, when Vanda grabbed a hold of her from behind and yanked at the slicker, Audrey immediately thought some of those boys had it in mind to have their way with her, which The Diner can not imagine what way that would be, Audrey being the size she is, and she let out a bloodcurdling shriek which could be heard throughout the gymnasium and for several blocks around, as it turned out, and certainly disconcerted those of us partaking of our repasts.

In the meantime, Lita Jane had tried to put out the fire with her apron, which had gone up in flames as well, and she admits that she must have lost her presence of mind at this point, and instead of running into the shower room—though in all fairness to her judgment, Audrey and Vanda were now rolling about on the floor there and flailing at one another, so she probably would have ended up knocked down just the same and might have taken a few body blows before things got straightened out—she came running ablaze and screaming into the dining room part of the gymnasium, with the wet and wild-eyed dog howling at her heels, and they ran smack into Zoe Pickerwell limping across the room with another armload of pancakes and one of the blue pitchers of maple syrup, which she admits she was not paying any heed to the ruckus behind her, as she was contemplating how to explain to her table of diners all about the mix-up with the pitchers, so they wouldn't have to summon her back later to question the blueberry syrup, as by now she was having trouble walking and wanted to save herself the extra trip.

Well, the upshot of all this was, the automatic sprinklers went off and ruined everybody's pancakes and waffles, and service was cancelled for the evening, to the dismay of a number of hungry patrons waiting in the bleachers to be seated, many of whom were chagrined because they had already bought their meal tickets and the policy was "no refunds."

"With food like this, you just can't be giving people refunds," Marybeth Overjohn explained to one and all, "because what good are left over pancakes to anybody, and the whole idea was to make money anyway?"

All in all, despite the various lawsuits that have been filed, including the small claims one which has been filed over those refunds, and which the Diner cannot comment on any of them as they are still unresolved, which means that for the time being everyone is gagged from talking about them so as not to influence a jury, The Diner feels that he can recommend the pancake supper with full enthusiasm and it will be served again next Sunday and every Sunday for the rest of this month, with an encore performance of Laci Coleman's dexterous baton feats, but Marsha Cole has announced that she is disinclined to accompany herself with humming and chooses not to repeat her sparkling entertainment until the Committee can find another hi-fi, and her contribution I'm sure will be sorely missed, as The Diner would still like to see her do a polka with her walker; and for all those who may be interested, and The Diner hopes that you are a plethora, please make observation of the fact that the supper will be held henceforth in the cafeteria, so that the Propane cooker will not be required, as it was destroyed in the fire anyway, along with much of the boy's shower room.

As a matter of passing interest, the Women's Club is looking for a good waitress. "You can't serve pancakes on crutches," Zoe Pickerwell told The Diner with her usual *joie de vivre*, when he interviewed her afterward at her abode. And Marybeth asks me to mention that they desperately need a *chef de pancakes* as well, since Lita Jane Jenson's hands are swathed in bandages for the time being "and I can't cook for beans," as Marybeth says. Fortunately, Vanda is back to acting as hostess, though she is wearing dark glasses as her eyes are still red from the pepper spray and she has a bandage on her left leg where Audrey bit her while they were tussling. Also, having been informed that Gour-may is now *persona non grata*, though I personally don't see how he can be blamed for any of the disorder, Audrey refuses to wash dishes in the future, and in fact has not ventured out of her house since and has taken to piling her furniture in front of her bedroom door when she retires at night, so they are seeking a volunteer for that chore, all of which, please remember, is for a good cause.

Until next week, this is the Underground Diner saying *Buon appetito*.

THE UNDERGROUND DINER
COLUMN FOR FRIDAY, JUNE 10
HIGH ON THE HOG

Since last week's column was devoted to a delicious but inexpensive pancake supper, The Diner thought this week he should write about one of the more elegant dining options in our fair city, or as a wit The Diner knows likes to put it, we decided we would go "high on the hog," which is an expression. So, after consulting with The Friend, The Diner decided upon the Lucky Pierre Dining Room at the Happy Deuce Motel which, as most of you already know, is on the north edge of town just off the interstate, and which, for the convenience of travelers, rents rooms by the hour as well as by the day, which causes it to be a very busy place and at mealtimes the dining room is nearly always crowded with truckers, business persons, and normal people enjoying a taste of *"haute cuisine,"* as we gourmets express it with one another.

Since it was only a few days from her birthday, the Diner invited The Friend's Mother along as well, and made a reservation for three for a 6:00 PM late dinner or, as some would call it, supper.

Because we were going someplace a bit more on the upscale side, The Diner and His Friend decided to dress appropriately. The Diner wore his string tie and a corduroy smoking jacket over a pair of freshly washed Levis, which The Friend even went so far as to iron for him, and which she even ironed in a pleat, and his expensive white snakeskin boots that were imported from San Antonio.

The Friend lamented that she didn't have a thing to wear, which The Diner knows will sound familiar to all of you husbands, and which she says every time they go anywhere, and there was the usual heated discussion of a shopping trip to Wal-Mart, but she eventually saw reason and came out of the bathroom, which The Diner thought it was just in time as he had been about to water the azaleas in the back yard; and she said that she had prayed on it and the answer had come to her out of the blue, that she would just wear her wedding dress, the color of which was what is called a royal white, which was where she got the idea while she was sitting on the throne, off of which she took the train, and she shortened the skirt a bit, and The Diner has to say, she looked just as lovely in it as she had the first seven times she had worn it.

The Mother made a joke that she was not going to dress up for some truckers' roadside pickup joint, and anyway she didn't have a wedding dress to make over, but then she gussied herself up to the nines in her toreador pants which are fire engine red and which you could have mistaken her for a fire engine from behind, but The Diner has better sense than to say something like that out loud; and worn with it was her zebra skin-looking top and enough rhinestones to practically blind you: these consisted of a pair of earrings that dangled just about to her shoulders, and her spectacles with the sparklers all around the frames, and not one but two necklaces, plus three bracelets, a brooch, and rings on every finger but her thumbs; and later I realized she was wearing an ankle bracelet too, so you can be sure that she looked very grand indeed, and The Diner admits his chest was puffed out to escort these two elegant ladies for a night on the town and he felt confident that no man there would be seen with anything like he was.

Our arrival at The Lucky Pierre (that is French, by the way, and is pronounced "pair," so it is a play on words, as you can see for yourself if you think about the name of the Motel, which is The Happy Deuce) was delayed when it was discovered that there was no ramp for the Mother's wheelchair, and for a time it looked as if birthday dinner might be at one of the nearby fast food operations which normally The Diner would eschew, being a gourmet, even though The Diner has observed that she can walk as well as the next one if she has a mind to, and to see her elbow her way to the front of the line when Penney's has a big sale and there are bargains to be had is a sight to behold; but the dilemma was solved when a long-distance trucker came to our rescue and, with the help of a passing businessman, graciously made a chair with their hands and carried The Mother inside, while The Diner and His Friend were able to tug the wheelchair up the steps. Unfortunately, we had already gotten it to the dining room before the manageress, one Miss Macilhenny, discovered us and explained that there was a wheelchair ramp at the main entrance, as we had come in through the motel lobby, which is beautifully decorated nevertheless with knobby pine and there is a sign over the check in counter that advises guests to please leave their values at the desk and another inviting the guests to please take advantage of the chambermaid if they needed anything, which The Diner thought made the place seem particularly welcome, as you don't always find that sort of accommodation these days.

All's well that ends well, however, so far as our perambulations into the dining room, and after a slight exchange of words between the long distance trucker and The Mother, who insisted that someone had taken liberties while she was being escorted inside, we settled ourselves at our table with its view of the interstate and a portion of the back parking lot with the colorful setting sun behind it, the beautiful view of which was unfortunately marred on this occasion by the sight of our same erstwhile long-distance trucker relieving himself near the rear of his truck and ignoring the honking of passing motorists. The Diner and The Friend quickly looked away when they saw what he was about, but The Mother was not so easily mollified and kept her eyes glued to him the entire time, to express her disapproval, as she put it.

The evening got off to an awkward start when the waitress, Maybelle June, as was said on the little name tag pinned to her impressive bosom, and which The Diner, whose eyesight is not what it once was, had to lean close and study carefully to read it, leaned over to set a drink on the table next to ours and had an escape of air from her bodily portion which was practically in our faces when she bent down, and she was most embarrassed and apologized profusely to us, but The Mother said, well, at least this week she wouldn't need to have her hair tinted, which would save her Twelve-Fifty, and anyway Blanche Ferguson never could get the color right, and maybe Maybelle June ought to go into the business. The Diner assured the young lady, whose name he had to take a second good look at, that it was the sort of thing that could happen to anybody, and he started to tell her about the time at his Aunt Minna's funeral, when he had bent over the casket to give his dear old Auntie a farewell kiss, and blew Uncle Ezra's hairpiece half way round on his head, so that the part went crossways and he had these bangs over his forehead; but The Friend said if he told that story one more time she was just going to get up and leave, and besides, she opined that she was sure she had read in Emily Post that it was disrespectful of the dead to eat bean soup before you went to a funeral; but The Diner said, he doubted that Aunt Minna had an opinion one way or the other on the business, though he did allow that Uncle Ezra had sworn off bean soup for the rest of his days.

The air having cleared after a bit, with some generous fanning by The Mother of her napkin, we proceeded to place our orders with Maybelle June, The Diner politely checking to make sure he had her name right, as there is nothing more embarrassing than calling someone one thing when it turns out they are another, and this is something he always takes great trouble over.

For refreshments, The Diner ordered a white wine spritzer. This being a festive occasion, he decided to splurge and asked that it be made with Canada Dry club soda in lieu of the "well" soda, though he was properly warned by Maybelle June that this would cost twenty-five cents extra. At our helpful server's suggestion, The Friend decided to try a Pepsi-Fruitti, which Maybarry Jane (who corrected The Diner immediately and so occasioned another reading of her label, which The Mother said at this rate we would soon be "bosom friends," which was an example of The Mother's ready wit) described as a tall glass of Pepsi garnished with cherry, orange, and pineapple slices, and a splash of soda, twenty-five cents extra for name soda, which was the bartender's own creation and which Maybelle June said was quite popular with their regulars and which we could easily see for ourselves, especially the attractively dressed young ladies sitting in a row at the bar who proved over the course of the evening to be close friends with a number of the truckers, this being the sort of establishment where shyness is quickly over-come and good fellowship rules. The Mother ordered a double shot of Jack, neat, with a beer chaser.

While we awaited our cocktails, we made note of the dining room's fine appointments, in particular the enormous chande-lier in the middle of the room in the shape of a wagon wheel, which motif was echoed by the stuffed leather horsey near the jukebox (which our server said, inasmuch as it was her birthday, The Mother was welcome to sit on while she had her cocktail if she would like, which the children often did, but which she declined when the busboys insisted they were unwilling to help her onto it without extra pay, to which she took umbrage because she felt that maybe they were casting aspersions regarding her weight and luckily she did not hear the remark about the "fire truck" which occasioned much snickering among them) and the enchanting little candle-holders on each table in the shape of a cowboy boot. The Diner personally thought that the plain white cloth napkins were a bit stark after last week's dressy red-and-white-checked paper ones, but except for that one disappoint-ment, the décor was deemed quite sophisticated for our small city, and most admired were the seats at each table, in the shape of a saddle, though they took some holding onto to keep from sliding, especially after the imbibing of a refreshment or two.

When our beverages were subsequently served to us, all of us declared them perfectly prepared. The Mother in particular was so pleased with hers that she sent her compliments to the bartender and immediately ordered a second one before she had taken more than a sip of the first and hadn't touched the beer yet at all.

Refreshments on hand, we turned to perusing the delicious menu. The Lucky Pierre prides itself on its continental menu, and The Diner and his guests found many temptations among its *à la Cartes*. There is also a salad bar, with various salad assortments, on the floor.

After determining that the salad bar cost the same regardless of how little or how much one partook of it, The Mother decided that she would just make do with a salad for her dinner, as she did not have much of an appetite. Plates were provided at the Salad bar, but on her way to fetch her salad The Mother passed a waiter's station and, seeing an unused tray there, decided she would just make do with that instead of one of those little bitty plates because as she explained it, that would reduce the load in the dishwasher and so save the establishment money, which the Diner admired her for her consideration of others, as not many people today do.

The Mother started her salad with three kinds of lettuce, including romaine, butter, and red leaf, which she bedded directly onto her tray, having first wiped it clean on the leg of her toreador pants to be safe, and she then garnished it with generous helpings of sliced tomato, little whole beets, those pickled tiny ears of corn, broccoli and cauliflower florets, navy beans, string beans and pinto beans, sliced cucumber (which she left some of that behind as it was all wilted), black and green olives, slices of red and green bell pepper, bacon crumbles, cheddar and blue cheese bits, anchovies, tuna fish, bread and butter pickles, plain and garlic croutons, sunflower seeds, scallions, little bitty cocktail onions, and diced chicken, boiled eggs and the whole red pickled ones, baby new potatoes with parsley, fried chicken livers, radishes and celery, and macaroni salad, which she dressed all of which with their House Italian dressing and added a large dollop of ranch on top of that "to meld the flavors," and some slices of thin-sliced deli ham, which she put to the side, as she preferred to keep her salads on the plain and simple style and she thought the ham might be *de trop.*

While The Mother was busy at the salad bar composing her salad, The Diner chose a Jumbo Shrimp Cocktail Pierre for a first course, which according to the menu was made with shrimp from The Waters of Mexico, which told him they were the underwater kind of shrimp, and which gave the dinner a true international cast, and he ordered the meatloaf with mashed potatoes and gravy and parsleyed carrots to follow. The Friend toyed with chicken fried steak, which is always a favorite of hers, but finally decided that maybe she didn't want anything that fancy, and she would just have a Deluxe Cheeseburger, which comes with pickle, lettuce, tomato and the Special Lucky Sauce, or mayonnaise if you prefer, plus your choice of cheese, on a whole wheat bun, with fries or onion rings on the side, which she ordered very well done, because she hates any pink in her hamburgers. She opined that she would just have a little green salad for her starter, but unfortunately when she got to the salad bar, she found that it had been stripped clean by the other diners and had not been restocked, so there was nothing there but a couple of slices of wilted looking cucumber, as she described it. The Diner would suggest to the management that someone should keep an eye on the salad bar in the future and make sure it is well equipped at all times, which is just a minor cavil that he would pass on to them.

When The Mother got back to the table—which took some doing because her salad was piled up to where she couldn't see over it and she had to keep peeking around the sides, and plus she had to negotiate around all those close-spaced tables and she bumped into one old lady so hard that she fell face down in her pumpkin bisque, which is similar to a soup, but by the time she got it out of her eyes, The Mother was gone and she did not know who to blame—she announced that she would not need a first course. "I will just have another Jack for an appetizer," was how she put it, and gave that perky little laugh of hers, which always brings a smile to the face of everyone who hears it and had the people sitting at the next table laughing out loud, as it is that kind of establishment where *bonhomie* rules.

The Diner's Jumbo Shrimp Cocktail Pierre was served in an enormous margarita glass, with lots of shredded lettuce in the bottom and a very tasty cocktail sauce, which Maybelle June informed me in a whisper, was Heinz. The shrimp were a little on the too-cold side, one of them not completely thawed out, but as it was a warm evening, particularly with the chandelier and all those candles in the cowboy boots ablaze, the cold and crunchy shrimp were particularly welcome, but The Diner has some reservations about whether they were truly the kind that grow under the water, as they tasted like the packaged freezer kind to him, and especially with that ice that made him suspicious.

The Mother was certainly relishing her salad by this juncture of the evening and was leaned over her tray with both hands moving like lightning, which is truly a sight to behold if you have never seen it, but she did say that she was off the beans after what had happened earlier, and besides the air at our table didn't need any more perfuming, and she just did not care to even have them on her plate at all as they were spoiling her appetite, but she couldn't see anyplace to put them as The Diner refused to have them added to his Jumbo Shrimp Cocktail Pierre, until she espied that the woman at the next table, who had been laughing the hardest of anybody, had left her purse sitting open on the floor by her chair leg. So The Mother rolled what was left of the beans up neatly in some slices of the deli ham, and pointed across the room and shouted, "I see what you are doing over there under that table," and when the lady stretched her neck to see, The Mother deftly slipped the ham and beans into the woman's purse and snapped it shut, which she had disposed of the problem neatly, she said, and ordered herself another Jack to celebrate her own cleverness, as she put it.

There was a bit of a brouhaha between courses (between my courses, that is to say, as The Friend had missed out on the little green salad she had meant to have as her first course, and The Mother was only having just her salad) when the manageress, Miss Macilhenny, showed up to complain that The Mother had disabused the salad bar, which wasn't meant to be partaken of on waiters' trays, and there was now a rather large crowd of diners milling about and poking at those wilted cucumber slices, which was all that was left.

The Diner could see that the manageress did indeed have a point about the waiter's tray, but as The Mother pointed out, our server, Maybelle June, had assured her that she could make as many trips as she liked to the salad bar, and as she was in a wheelchair and it was inconvenient for her to be scurrying back and forth every few minutes, which would have been a lot easier if they had placed the salad bar somewhere closer to our table and not halfway across town, and what difference did it make if she got it all at once and saved herself the trouble? Anyhow, as she put it, she thought the salad bar had abused itself, as the cucumbers were wilted, which The Friend was willing to attest to, and the deviled eggs had been so long out of the nest that they wouldn't have recognized their own mother's *patootie*.

Which Miss Macilhenny replied to with a rude suggestion that concerned her own *patootie*, and The Mother retorted that Miss Macilhenny was so dumb she wouldn't know the south end of a chicken going north, and there is no telling where this conversation would have gotten to, but it was culminated when The Mother accidentally rolled the wheel of her chair over Miss Macilhenny's toes, this being the danger of wearing open-toed shoes in a job as physical as hers was, and when Miss Macilhenny began to shriek and flail about with her arms, The Mother got disconcerted and ran back and forth several more times over the toes before she got her senses back, and by this time considerable damage had been done, including dumping

The Diner's Jumbo Shrimp Cocktail Pierre into his lap which necessitated his eating the rest of it from there, and which caused some other diners to give him peculiar looks, but at a dollar ninety-eight before seven PM, he was not about to waste a good shrimp cocktail, and besides the levis had just been washed and ironed, including a pleat.

The busboys rushed up to help Miss Macilhenny away, and since she was of an ample size, they hoisted her onto the leather horsey and carried it through the dining room, which The Mother said was the first time she had ever seen a horse with two hind-ends, and she further opined that Miss Macilhenny was the only thing there older than the macaroni salad, and the woman at the next table got to laughing so hard at The Mother's witticisms that she reached in her purse for a hankie and now she was wiping her eyes with a slice of deli him.

The Mother however, pronounced herself "downright ticked off" at being treated like a second-class citizen, and out of spite she scraped the rest of her salad onto the floor under the table, the pickled eggs of which landed on one of The Diner's white snakeskin boots and stained the toe of one of them bright pink, which he tried to get off with the corner of the tablecloth, but to no avail, and The Friend said probably he would just have to dye the other one to match, but The Diner said he could not very well go around wearing pink boots because what would people think, and The Friend said that was a laugh coming from a man who liked to wear women's panties, and The Diner said she didn't have to trumpet everything she knew for all the world to hear, since the woman at the next table was now all bent over laughing and was trying to blow her nose on a string bean, and anyway, he only wore the panties when he and The Friend were engaged in some romantic interludes, and The Friend said she didn't see anything romantic about a man in pink panties with Love Will Come embroidered across the front of them, and that was the only thing that did most times anyway.

The Mother, who is nothing if not fastidious, said she had had enough of this kind of gutter talk, and she drove herself back to the salad bar with her tray, which was now being hastily restocked by a half dozen busboys.

Well, it seems Miss Macilhenny's foot was being treated at the hostess counter with bacon grease on her toe, because some people say that is good for an open wound like hers, and the grease was being applied to the wound by one of the chefs, which The Diner must admit was pretty ugly, and Miss Macilhenny saw The Mother aiming for the salad bar again, and she had barely gotten a fork into the pickled tomatoes, though as she said afterward, she'd have gotten there in plenty of time if she hadn't "out of the kindness of my heart" stopped on her way past one of the tables when a woman complained that there was a bug in her potato salad and The Mother said, "if you think that's bad, you ought to see the mess on the floor under our table," and from the way she described it, three people got up to come and see for themselves, and they were shocked, but none of them had any suggestions for getting the pickled egg stain off the snakeskin boot, so I guess that will just be a loss, and also by this time the woman at the next table had gotten herself into such a lather that she had slid right off her saddle chair and which she was laughing so hard she couldn't get up to make it to the bathroom so this was another mess on that floor, which the visitors took note of, and the fact that the woman was wearing beans all down the front of her dress, which all agreed was an unusual fashion statement.

But I have gotten off the sidetrack here, and to recapitulate, however, when Miss Macilhenny saw The Mother making her comeback at the salad bar, she snatched a fire extinguisher off the wall and came charging across the room after her, and The Diner has to say, she was moving pretty good for a hefty woman hopping on one foot which if you have never done it is not easy to do and shoot someone in the face with a fire extinguisher while you are at it.

Needless to say, The Mother did not take kindly to a face full of foam, which she said left such a bad taste in her mouth that she was off her feed for a week, and she snatched a crutch right out from under an old codger who had the misfortune to pass by at that very moment, and who in his unbalance toppled across a table full of people who were just dishing around their All-You-Can-Eat-Spaghetti-Platter-for-a-Family-of Six, which sent spaghetti flying everywhere and they thought that he had been stricken of a coronary, and there was lots of screaming, and someone dialed 9-1-1 and reported a man had just died at the restaurant, and the 9-1-1 woman said, "Oh, not there again," and told them someone would be there by and by, and never to order the Tunafish Special Surprise at that place, if she had only known ahead of time, she would have been sure to warn them, and the health department ought to put up a sign about that, if you asked her.

Meanwhile, The Mother was stabbing Miss Macilhenny in the belly with the tip end of the crutch to keep her at bay, and one of the ladies at the table across which the old codger had toppled, thinking that he needed reviving, was attempting to give him mouth breathing, and he thought, as he explained later, that she had simply been overcome with a fit of passion and was trying to have her way with him, though why he should have thought that The Diner had no idea, since he wasn't but a scrawny stick of a thing anyway, but it is always those fellows who think they are God's gift, as The Friend points out, and he was trying to fend her off and his wife, who had taken good notice of those young ladies at the bar and thought that perhaps this one had started her evening at that location, was whacking at her with his other crutch, which she had outfought The Mother for, and he had just attained to his hands and knees in the spaghetti sauce when Miss Macilhenny, who had managed by now to hoist herself up atop the salad bar to get a better shot at The Mother, stepped into the new container of cottage cheese which the busboys had just replaced, with her good foot and went sailing, and lighted right astride the same poor fellow's back, and he was so overwhelmed by being assaulted with not one but two amorous females, as he thought it, that he fainted dead away, and the mouth breather was at him again, to the additional dismay of the wife, who took off a high heeled shoe to replace the crutch which Miss Macilhenny's spectacular descent had knocked to the floor and which The Mother was now wielding two of, which gave her a good advantage in the weaponry, the fire extinguisher having stayed behind amongst the pickled beets.

Now, The Diner is not one to point fingers, because as it says in the Good Book, let him who is without rocks cast the first stone, but he does hold of the opinion that what happened subsequently belongs right at the foot of that 9-1-1 operator, because she admitted when everything came out later that she had her mind just full up with that Tunafish Special Surprise, which she said was surely a surprise all right, and which had caused her three calls in the last month alone and she was just plain aggravated about, and she had just gotten a call as well of an illegal bingo game at Saint Alfonso of the Valley Church, and she got the addresses mixed up, so instead of the paramedics, we got the raiding party and the paramedics went to the church, which worked out just fine for them, because two of them came out winners, and the Pastor said he had never seen newcomers with such luck and he hoped that they put at least a little something into the poor box before they left, which only one of them did so.

When the raiding party came in, The Mother showed how fast she could move when she wanted to, and she abandoned her wheelchair, which was covered by now in fire extinguisher foam anyway and she put in a claim the next day for a new one, and where it asked the cause of the damage, she said she had met up with a cow which the agency said had never happened before in that neck of the woods, and she hightailed it back to our table, and the police officers, seeing three women on top of a table in what looked like a gang assault upon the person of an unconscious and helpless man, they arrested Miss Macilhenny and the mouth breather and the wife all three, and they took the codger with them for good measure, because as the Vice Captain, Vernon Melon, said to The Diner when he identified himself as a Gentleman of the Press, he might have been feigning unconsciousness to egg them on. "Some of these old coots can be pretty cagey," as he put it in a nutshell, and also arrested was the woman from the table next to ours as well, even though Captain Melon admitted as to how he wasn't sure what she had been up to, but as he put it, there was something awful suspicious about a person lying in a puddle of pee on the floor of a restaurant that has a string bean sticking out of her nose and can't stop laughing long enough to give you any kind of explanation for things.

In summation, The Diner can tell you that the service is mostly pretty good at the Lucky Pierre and if you go, ask for Maybelle June, and be sure to get a good look at her name tag, which you will find impressive, he is certain; and the food was fine, though the mashed potatoes that eventually arrived with his meat loaf, which were Betty Crocker, had been made with two much water and were more of a puddle than a mound, as the menu put it, but he recommends that you skip the salad bar, because of those wilted cucumbers, and as The Mother warned, they probably were just going to serve that cottage cheese again regardless of how many filthy feet had been in it.

Albeit, nonetheless, the evening was pronounced a success by our little trio, and The Mother said she hadn't had so much fun in a dog's age, though The Diner thinks she was probably more uproarious over the sight of Miss Macilhenny being removed from the premises in handcuffs, hopping on one foot and trailing spaghetti sauce, than she was over the cuisine.

We did not get to have dessert, however, because the police closed up the place for the night for illegal bingo, though the officers were still searching for clues, in pursuit of which two or three of them had accompanied some of those young ladies from the bar to their rooms at the motel to look for evidence, so he is confident that whatever was afoot has been apprehended due to the efficiency of our local police department, and The Diner was assured that the restaurant will be open again by the following night, and he thinks that you should pay a visit the next time a special occasion causes you to have the urge.

To coin a phrase, The Underground Diner wishes you all *Bon Appetite*.

THE UNDERGROUND DINER
COLUMN FOR FRIDAY, JUNE 17
CRUISIN' DOWN THE RIVER

Having enjoyed the last couple of weeks a dress-up dinner at the Lucky Pierre Restaurant and an *al fresco* pancake supper the week before that, The Diner's Friend suggested that this week being summer, it would be pleasant to eat someplace out-of-doors, and The Diner immediately thought of the perfect spot, with the river and the pine trees wafting their scents while they lapped at our feet, and when she heard where we were headed, The Friend's Mother invited herself to join us, as she had had such a bang-up time last week at The Lucky Pierre, and The Diner hopes that you all read and enjoyed his tales of our culinary expedition to that fine eating establishment. And also, we thought it a good idea to get away from the house for a spell, as we had been plagued of late by some anonymous and nasty calls, the gist of which was someone wished we would get out of town, and of which there were other, more colorful suggestions, too, which some of them, The Diner is sure, being medically impossible, and we had reasoned that this was some crackpot who had gotten loose and had the bad luck to settle on The Diner and it would be good to get away from for an evening, as that phone wouldn't stop.

So in no time at all the three of us were installed in the Jimmy and inasmuch as The Mother was temporarily without her wheelchair, which would take this whole column to explain but was the result of an unfortunate mishap that had happened of late, The Diner put the old Barcalounger from the garage, which the dogs were used to sleeping on and which they looked forlornly after it when it headed out the door, into the back of the Jimmy and as there is no seat belts back there and the law says you have to be strapped in, he tied a piece of clothesline around The Mother to make sure she didn't fly out of the pickup bed, and she opined as she was quite comfortable back there even though all that dog hair, and besides she could blow kisses at the truckers as we went by, which she must have done more than that, as one of them ran clear off the road craning his neck, and she said that was The Diner's own fault, because if he hadn't been driving like a bat out of Sandusky, it wouldn't have blown her gypsy blouse clear over her head, as it fitted loose to begin with and she had never been so embarrassed in her life, having everyone on the interstate ogling her private uppers.

How it happened was, we were on the two-lane and crawling along behind this truck, and The Diner edged up close and he had a sign on his tail end that said, "I May Be Slow But I Am Ahead Of You, Sucker", and The Friend said, if that didn't tick her off, and just to go right on around him, why didn't we, and as we were on a hill and couldn't see if there was traffic coming, so to be safe, The Diner passed him on the shoulder of the road, which the ditch there wasn't real deep anyway, and with The Mother's blouse over her head, all that bouncing had her upper members moving something fierce, as she put it, and that is when the trucker went off the road on the other side, and he came right over a highway patrolman's motorcycle, which the officer was waiting to catch himself some speeders, and he leaped clear off that bike just in time when he saw that truck headed at him.

Well, The Diner pulled over of course to see if he could help that trucker and the police officer, and the mother insisted on being untied to help too, but when the two men saw us coming they abandoned their vehicles and lit out across a corn field, the trucker being in the lead but the officer making pretty good time himself for a man with a limp, which the mother said probably they had to go real bad and didn't want to do it there by the roadside, which she said thinking of those two made her have to go on top of all that bouncing, inasmuch as that would shake the water out of a cactus, and their running off like that did not deter her in the least because as she said, if the passersby didn't want to see, they didn't have to look, and she couldn't wait to go running across a corn field to try to find a euphemism, which The Diner said it would save the weed control people a spray trip anyway.

Well, when that business was attended to and everyone was tied back in their place, which The Mother wasn't speaking to The Diner after his remark about the weeds, we headed on down the road for Fred and June's Dew Drop Inn Live Bait Shop and Luncheonette, which as many of you know is on a houseboat located at the end of Old Possum Hunt Trail, which was the two lane we were on, on the very banks of the river, which the sun was near to setting upon by the time we savored the crunch of gravel under our tires.

Fred and June's Dew Drop Inn Live Bait Shop and Luncheonette is a casual dining experience, and the three of us had dressed accordingly, The Mother of course in that blouse that wouldn't stay put and her brown mohair Capri pants which when she walked looked like two groundhogs wrestling, and the rest of us were in sundresses and tee shirts, the former of which The Friend had donned and The Diner was in the latter, in case you might have had a peculiar picture in your minds, as The Diner would not want anyone to get the wrong idea, especially after some certain remarks that someone had made publicly to one and all on our last outing, and The Friend wore her Peek-a-Boo blouse, of which she said laughing that she hoped somebody might peek, and I said I just hoped they didn't say boo, and she did not talk to him on the journey either, which The Diner privately thanked the Lord for small blessings.

We were greeted at the door by a perky Almondine Crumpet, who both of them recognized one another as she and The

Mother had gone to school together, but Almondine is years older, as The Mother is ever at pains to point out, the reason being that she was one of fifteen Crumpets and when she was a child, Almondine decided her first day of school that she wasn't interested in any more of it and so when the other Crumpets trooped off to school each day she hid in the cow barn and it wasn't until she was twelve that her mother caught sight of her one day in the chicken yard and immediately recognized her for who she was, and Almondine was carted off to school that very day and kept there, but she was already old for her age, and she was twenty-four by the time she graduated, though of course she got older as the years passed, and the two of them never were friendly.

Almondine asked if we were there to fish or dine, and The Mother said the only thing she fished for anymore was compliments, and Almondine said that she might want to think about changing her bait, which it was not until later that The Mother decided was on the snippy side, and The Diner could have warned the person that it was not the best business to get on the wrong side of The Mother, but then he thought, each to his own, as the man said when he kissed the cow, and anyhow, once The Mother got it into her head that she was not pleased with Almondine, she forgot that she was ticked off at The Diner, which the repast to ensue would surely be more pleasant for it.

Unbeknownst to the ladies, The Diner had called ahead and arranged for a surprise, and we were reserved for Fred and June's Special Romantic Moonlight Dinner Cruise and Musicale, which consisted of we got into Fred's outboard, which includes a one-hundred-horsepower Mercury engine, and we were paraded up and down the river while Fred's nephew Dickie, who learned music at the community college and is locally recognized as an authentic real singer except he does walk somewhat funny, which we wouldn't notice however in the boat, serenades you with befitting operatic music like "Blow The Man Down" and "Indian Love Call", but sadly it turned out that Dickie had been stricken with some errant crockery a week earlier at a pancake supper, and it had left his windpipe out of commission for singing, which The Diner did wonder where the crockery had caught him, and he was not available for the evening, and The Diner said he ought to have been informed of that when he made his reservation, which he had guaranteed with his Chevron card which you have to do in advance to arrange for the Special Romantic Moonlight Dinner Cruise and Musicale, and if we were not getting the whole package, there ought to be an allowance made on the price, and we were at a stalemate for a bit, until June said she had found somebody to sing in Dickie's place, being one of the other patrons there for the evening.

Well, it turned out to be our old friend, Zoe Pickerwell, who said it was just making her feet itch all that good music playing on the jukebox and her not able to dance on account of her crutches, and especially Jailhouse Rock, which she said reminded her of her first beau, and The Friend said out of the corner of her mouth that she would have bet on "The Battle Hymn of the Republic", which got The Mother laughing so hard that she had been drinking a beer which came from the cooler, and the beer came out her nose and three people got up from the lunch counter, which was two long boards which Fred had placed across his rear end on sawhorses, and they left and Fred had to go after them because one of them hadn't paid for his Catfish and Hominy Plate, and Zoe said she might as leave go sit on the front end of the boat and sing for us, as she did in church on Sundays anyway, and at least she wouldn't have to wear a choir robe, which she always does in church even when it is hotter than blazes, because as she said, the Lord apparently didn't believe in air-conditioning for the New Albany Baptist Assembly, which The Mother, who is as devout as the next one, reminded her of Daniel in the lions' den after the blowing of her nose, and Zoe said Daniel didn't have to wear a choir robe and if he had, those lions might have had something to get their teeth into, and The Mother served her opinion that such a testament was blasphemous, and Zoe said if The Mother thought she was so blasphemous, maybe she would just stay right inside by the jukebox and listen to Elvis and The Mother could sing for her own self, and it looked as if the River Cruise might be spoiled for the Musicale portion of it, but Almondine Crumpet came by at just that fortuitous moment to take our orders. Well, The Mother ordered The Bumble Bee Tuna Spaghetti Bucket, of which she hoped Miss Strumpet could keep her fingers out of the bucket, and Almondine said that who was she calling a strumpet, and The Mother said that she didn't understand why she was looking so huffy as she had plainly and clearly said Miss Crumpet, and maybe somebody's hearing was going, which Zoe Pickerwell said, that happens sometimes when a body gets on in years, and the two of them got to laughing so hard that the beer came out of The Mother's nose again and Zoe said she was in danger of leaking and if they didn't stop she'd have to go drape herself over the edge of the houseboat and there would just be an early moon above the river, and the two of them once again embraced the sacred bonds of friendship, though Almondine Crumpet wasn't so very tickled, and went off to the kitchen in a high dudgeon.

Fred has a sign posted next to the boat that says, "You must be twenty-one to ride this boat, or under an adult," which is because of the romantic nature of the cruise, which The Diner thought the romantics would be curtailed a bit with The Mother along, but the ride would be nice anyway.

The Way Fred and June's Special Moonlight Dinner Cruise and Musicale works, you place your dinner order before your boat sails, but you take your beverages along. As The Diner can attest, who is an old salt from way back, it can get plenty dry out there on the main, and then you come back to the dock to get your dinners, because there would not be room in the outboard to set up a table properly, as it was barely room enough for us as it was, with Fred at the back manning the engine, and Zoe at the front end with her crutches laid out long ways, and the cooler with our drinks, and Fred had bought his fishing pole along in the chance that he might catch something for the kitchen, and also on board were The Diner and The Friend and The Mother, who laughed gaily and said maybe she should just sit on Fred's lap, which he said he needed his hands and his feet both to manipulate the controls, and which The Diner watched for all evening but never did see him use his feet until that unfortunate incident towards the end of things, and June, who was casting us off, said anyway the motor wouldn't work if it was completely underwater from too much weight at one end, which is certainly the case, as except for submarines, boats weren't designed to work underwater and you couldn't do a moonlight dinner cruise in a submarine, since you wouldn't get much moonlight. The Mother said it was a good thing June wasn't going along or the whole boat would be under. And June said something in reply, but Fred gunned the motor at that moment which we couldn't hear what was said and we set sail without further ado.

If The Diner may be permitted to back up here, there is a generous selection of beverages to choose from before setting sail, including coffee and tea and just about any kind of soda pop you could think of. The Friend selected the Hot Tea Your Way as it is described on the wall menu (which is the clean side of the back of a cardboard box with the selections written in red nail polish, which The Friend, who is of an artistic nature, described as completely clever), which consists of a little metal pot of warm water ("all the refills from the thermos that you want") and your choice of tea bags, the selection including Lipton black tea and Bigelow green tea and Celestial Seasons Mandarin Orange; which is served with any one of three elegant plastic cups, the choices being Wile Coyote, Snoopy, or Sylvester the Cat. The Friend chose the Wile Coyote with The Mandarin Orange teabag, which she pronounced produced an oriental tea experience appropriate to a cruise and made her feel that she had traveled to some exotic location, which was enhanced by the river view with The Holiday Inn across the way, and the coal barges.

The Diner chose a Pepsi, which normally is imbibed directly from the can, but which he persuaded Almondine to let him have the Snoopy cup, which regardless of The Mother's disdain, showed that the staff in this fine establishment was there to please their customers, and you don't find service like that just any old place these days, as The Diner is well acquainted.

Also available for those on a budget is plain water, which some people apparently feared that Fred just hauled directly out of the river, so that there was a big sign as you came in that assured them that the management had personally passed all the water that was served in the establishment.

The Mother said she would just have a brewski, and as the cruise was to last the better part of half an hour they could just throw a couple of spares in the cooler as well, and Fred warned against drinking heavy when afloat and The Mother said she didn't think three beers constituted drinking heavy, and The Friend said what about that little flask of Jack that she kept tucked into the waist band of her knickers, and The Mother said people didn't have to shout everything they knew for the world to hear and what about that conversation the previous week about The Diner's panties, which Fred was curious about but The Diner said never mind, because he had disposed of them anyway and The Friend said that was too bad because she had told the ladies at her bridge club all about them and several of them had wanted to see and she had promised to bring them the following Thursday for show-and-tell, and now they would have to settle for the Polaroids, of which the Diner had not known.

Well, the moonlight cruise started off all right, except that it wasn't yet moonlight, but Fred said, he could hardly run that boat up and down the river in the dark could he, which the Diner had to agree with. We hadn't gone more than a few feet from the dock, though, when the subject came up of what Zoe was going to sing, as she said she didn't know a lot of songs without a songbook, and most of what she did know were hymns, and none of us could work up much enthusiasm for "Nearer My God to Thee", being as we were asea and no one could forget what happened to *The Hindenburg*, although Fred said he was pretty sure there were no icebergs in the neighborhood.

The Mother said if it was going to be "Row, Row, Row Your Boat", which you couldn't do justice to without singing parts, and if she had to sing too she wanted a piece of the money, which Zoe said she wasn't getting paid except with a large pizza, and The Mother was welcome to a piece of that if she liked.

So we settled finally for "She'll Be Coming 'Round the Mountain", which The Diner can say Zoe sang with great enthusiasm and he soon enough thought he had a pretty good idea what the people at that church of hers were probably praying for on Sundays, and apparently the two fishermen in the nearby boat felt the same, as they started yelling at her to cut out that caterwauling as she was scaring the fish away, and Zoe replied by singing louder, and just for spite The Mother joined in with her though she said she would pass on that pizza, and I heard later from people up to the North that they thought an early spawning season had begun as there were so many fish hastening upstream, one of whom had called the university to send their experts to take a look.

Well, the men in the fishing boat kept hollering and Zoe and The Mother kept singing louder and The Mother was keeping time with one of her fingers aloft in the air so that, as she explained it, she could keep her and Zoe together, which made for better harmony.

The singing and The Mother's keeping time apparently motivated one of the fishermen to stand up in their boat and add to the water in the river, and The Mother intervened with herself to say, couldn't he see that Fred was fishing and he might be watering directly on somebody's dinner, and he yelled back to ask what was Fred using a pole for anyway, if The Mother stuck her face under the water the fish would surely jump right out of it, and she said she had half a mind to swim right over there and show him a thing or two, and he said she could have stopped the sentence half way through it, and The Mother was in danger of climbing into the water, but The Friend said she thought that much of the ambience had been subtracted from the atmosphere and she would just as leave head back to port as to go around that mountain one more time, which was what we did.

When we got back to the houseboat, however, The Friend and The Mother hadn't any more than climbed up that little ladder up to the dock and The Diner was trying to help Zoe with her leg in the cast, and Fred was still tying up our boat, and Almondine Crumpet came running out with a plastic bucket to say that The Mother's Bumble Bee Tuna Spaghetti Bucket was just now ready and why didn't she eat it while it was good and hot, and The Mother remarked that some people seemed to have remembered their manners it was good to see, and she would be polite and wait till the rest of us was served as well, but she thought she would just have a bite to see how it was, and she hadn't any more than gotten a good forkful of it when she let out a shriek and said that her spaghetti was alive, whereupon Almondine clapped a hand over her mouth and said, oh, my goodness, wasn't she just the silliest thing, she must have gotten the spaghetti mixed up with someone's live bait order, and The Mother was so mad she shoved Almondine right off the dock, so that she fell across the boat and being the bigger of the two, capsized it as well as knocking Zoe into the water, who was screaming help me, help me, I am drowning, to Fred, who was occupied with trying to save that Mercury engine and he replied that the water just there wasn't but three feet deep and she could easily wade ashore, and Zoe said was he forgetting she was in a cast which he said that engine had cost him two hundred dollars off of old Sam Pennywaite plus a month of free dinners and that Sam Pennywaite could eat enough catfish for six people and he thought he was slipping it into his pocket when his back was turned and taking it home for later, and he would bet a dollar to a doughnut that her cast wasn't worth anywhere near that.

Well, Almondine wasn't willing to let well enough alone, and didn't she just reach up and grab The Mother's ankles, where she was standing on the dock laughing herself silly, and she ended up in the water with her, and the two of them began to have at it with a vengeance, which The Diner could have warned Almondine against trying to wrestle with that woman, as last year in Florida at the wild animal park The Mother had partaken of a considerable quantity of Jack which she had cleverly disguised in a Pepsi can, and when the alligator wrestling display was slow to get off the ground, she climbed right into the reptile pit, and the alligators seeing how fired up she was and having better sense it seems than Almondine, refused to wrestle with her to a man, and she had to settle for chasing them round and round the pit, which the spectators were cheering and egging her on, and one old lady was so worked up she toppled over the railing right into the pit and was run over by three alligators and The Mother before she knew what had happened, and the oldest of them was getting winded and losing ground and was wearing a pitiful fearsome expression before the security guards fetched The Mother out of there. They left the old lady to climb out herself, as the alligators had no use for her, being so winded, and the park had to close the exhibit for most of a week because the gators would do nothing but lay on their bellies and give the tourists the fish-eye, and which Almondine must have realized for herself after a time, so for a diversion she settled for snatching The Mother's artificial Zircon pendant from around her neck and giving it a toss, where it landed in the branches of one of the pine trees.

Now, The Mother was in a complete meltdown over what she called "this act of perfidy," as she had spent thirty-nine ninety-nine for that pendant at K-Mart on sale, which it would have been forty-nine ninety-nine regular, and she says she would have held Almondine's head under the water till the bubbles quit, but she was too worried about that Zircon, before some crow spotted it and hauled it off, as everyone knows that they are attracted to sparkly things. So she settled for snatching a hold of a big old catfish which had come downstream against the traffic to investigate what all the thrashing around was about, and went to smack Almondine with that fish, who ducked and she catfished Zoe instead, where she was trying to climb up the ladder to the dock and knocked her back into the water again, so The Mother then spotted that plastic bucket of fish bait floating close by and she grabbed hold of that and dumped it over Almondine's head, which she screamed and sobbed about profusely as it took her the most fearsome gyrations to get all those worms out of her hair which had the water whipped up to a genuine froth and she had just spent forty dollars at Blanche Ferguson's beauty salon for a perm and Blanche wouldn't give her another one for six weeks in case her hair should fall out, worms or no worms.

Well, The Mother hightailed it up the ladder and out of the water and she knocked Zoe off the ladder in her haste where she was trying to haul herself up again, and headed straight for the pick-up, out of which the big chain saw was retrieved, and she fired that sucker up and set upon that pine tree with a vengeance, the idea of which was bringing it down so she could fetch her artificial Zircon pendant out of the branches where she could not have climbed up to if it was standing, and June came out of the houseboat hollering that the law was on its way and she had best stop if she knew what was good for her, as those pine trees were private property and The Mother said she would stop when June shinnied up that tree and got her pendant, and otherwise it was going to be private firewood before she was done.

Well, it didn't take Sheriff Abernathy any time at all to get there, as he was already out on Old Possum Hunt Trail investigating an accident with a truck and a Highway Patrolman's motorcycle, about which The Diner thought it sagacious to keep mum, and when he saw what The Mother was about, he told her to cease and desist and just to give him that chain saw.

Now, The Diner has to say, there was talk later that The Mother had surrendered to violence right off the bat, but as The Diner was a witness, she was right along trying to maintain a dialogue with the Sheriff and saying, "Come on, come on," and "you silly old...." which she said a word The Diner cannot write in a family newspaper and which was surely an exaggeration anyway, as the Sheriff is a married man with children and The Diner has never heard anything about him along those lines except for those same tired old stories and which out of decency The Diner would never venture to even hint at to anybody, and besides, as The Diner sees it, it is just plain undemocratic to hold it against somebody that he liked to dress up in his Mommy's clothes when he was a child as lots of little fellers do, and which he swears was given up entirely on the night of his thirty seventh birthday after that unfortunate incident out at the highway rest stop and which The Diner is not going to be guilty of circulating, because his lips were sworn to be sealed and he sincerely regrets having let the story slip over the course of an evening to The Mother, as he might have known you couldn't seal her lips with Elmer's glue.

Well, the Sheriff got so fired up over what she had called him that he said if she didn't surrender her weapon, as he called it, he would have to come over there and straighten her out, and she told him he could have that chain saw, all right, and she took it out of the tree and set off after him, and the Sheriff having a gun but which he cannot use as the noise makes him flinch and he is as likely to shoot his own foot as somebody else, and knowing a bad situation when he saw one, he took off running, and she chased him around and around that tree, and she says she would have caught him for sure only she was wearing those big old platform boots that all the kids wear today and they slowed her down some, as he had time to jump into his Sheriff's car and lock all the doors, inspiring her to take at the windshield posts with her chain saw, and he got excited and slipped the car into gear, only he put it in reverse instead of drive, and he backed lickety-split into that pine tree she had been sawing at, which it was his mistake that caused it to go over the wrong way, as The Mother had been cutting it right all along, having worked one summer in a lumberjack camp, and those boys had said time and time again that it had been a Godsend having her there because it surely made the time go a whole lot faster having a willing soul to take care of all those things for them that they had to do for themselves beforehand.

Well, with that nudge from the Sheriff's car, the tree came

down all right, and in the wrong direction, and it came down right across the houseboat which up to that time had been Fred and June's Dew Drop Inn Live Bait Shop and Luncheonette, out of which luckily June and the remaining patrons had already escaped, fearing what might happen, and so luckily no one was hurt with the exception of Zoe Pickerwell, who had finally managed to get out of the river and was so plum tuckered out as she put it that she just laid down on the dock to rest, and a branch of the tree caught her on her good leg, which now she has two casts, but all was not a total defeat, however, as The Mother was able to sift through the tree branches and she found her Zircon pendant.

Alas, The Diner cannot recommend this fine establishment for a dinner as he otherwise happily would, as it is now underwater and Fred and June are living in a tent, and are unable to fix anyone meals, although they are still offering bait for those who want to fish, and for those of you who are, I recommend it. And as some of you have asked about Almondine Crumpet, I am happy to relate that the doctors are optimistic, but Blanche Ferguson cannot be persuaded to give her a perm for another six weeks, on account of her hair, and The Mother says she sends her regrets.

Until next week, this is The Underground Diner, wishing you good eats.

THE WALTONSBERG WEST
PANHANDLE EXPRESS (II)

To Our Readers:

The Underground Diner, whom many of you know and love anonymously, has been asked to put his food and restaurant column on hiatus, during which time it will not be published, owing to a number of lawsuits that are pending, and also in response to some vicious threats that have been made by parties unknown and which have resulted in unpleasantness for all concerned, including The Diner himself.

During this time, The Diner will be assigned to a news desk and he will be writing normal pieces for this newspaper, which he intends to eschew the national and international events which he is sure is of less interest to our readers than it is to him, and which don't concern us the way our neighbors do. He intends instead to write enlightening and entertaining pieces for the weekly supplement, Miner Matters, of events and places of particular interest to our local populage.

All of which is to say that for the nonce, The Underground Diner will be The Underground Reporter. He wishes to thank you all for your hearty support, and to assure everyone that he is eager to return to eating, and letting you know all about it.

THE UNDERGROUND REPORTER
COLUMN FOR OCTOBER 28
MINER MATTERS—THE SLEEP WELL FUNERAL PARLOR AND MORTUARY

Our motto is, "We want to make your grief memorable."

OCTOBER 28—The Underground Reporter was alive when he visited the Sleep Well Mortuary this past week, but he is sure that he could not have enjoyed it any more if he were dead. Certainly, he would be equally impressed with the fine appointments and the commitment to excellence that he found when he investigated this long time family business for our readers.

Funeral Home Manager Earl Digger pronounced himself delighted to meet with The Reporter and spared no effort to show him around and to explain the fine points of their important business.

For starters, there are three separate viewing rooms which can seat anywhere from ten to fifty mourners in comfort, and all of which are beautifully decorated in various motifs. The Mountain Living Room, for instance, is furnished in log furniture with knobby pine walls and rag rugs on the floor, and might have been a parlor in someone's lovely home, except for the casket display at the front of the room, which you would be unlikely to find in your average home. There is a Flying High Room, which is cleverly decorated to look like the interior of a Boeing 747 Airliner, even to the oxygen masks that drop down over the seats as they play the recessional, and The Dance Away the Night Room which has disco lights and a dance stage that can be erected right over the casket. "Some people relieve their grief in physical activity," Digger explained, "and this room has been popular not only for memorial services but for private party rentals."

Each of the rooms is equipped with state of the art hi-fi systems and there is an enormous catalog of music that guests can choose from. "Our most popular selection," Diggers explained, "Is Patsy Cline's 'Crazy'." People find that comforting, which is well understood by The Reporter.

The Sleep Well has a wide range of service options which can accommodate almost any family's needs and budget, and which are presented in the form of a menu after the style of the popular Hamburger Heaven for perusal by The Reporter and those who are interested.

Digger points out The Entry Level Service, which features a good, sturdy cardboard box, "And you won't find anything better than that for Two hundred dollars, you can bet your booty, and unlike with another mortuary service across town, of which he will not name, with our entry level, the deceased actually gets buried in the box in the ground, only, of course, just not as deeply as with some of the more expensive option, since people have to be paid a pretty penny to dig those holes, especially in the winter. As to those ugly rumors of dogs and raccoons digging up bits and pieces, that is just plain false as can be, although a groundhog did choose to make his nest with one of the retirees last season, but there are probably some who would be glad for the company," he said with a hearty laugh. Indeed, one of the things that impressed The Reporter the most was the ceaseless joie de vivre on display everywhere, which should help to brighten the funerary experience for any and all.

Everything on the menu is currently available with the exception of the Cake and Ice Cream Service, which had to be suspended because of an unfortunate incident which occurred when it was last occasioned. What this was, the lights in the chapel are dimmed, and candles are lighted, one for each year of the deceased's life on a cake, which is home made from the Bon Ton Bakery across town, and it is carried into the room with great ceremony by the local girl scouts while Zoe Pickerwell sings "So Long, It's Been Good to Know You," from the hall outside (which, personally, The Reporter thinks that anyone who has heard Zoe sing "She'll Be Comin' 'Round the Mountain," will surely have lost their fear of death, but he kept that opinion to himself, as it is not polite to mock someone who is in two casts owing to some unfortunate dining experiences.)

What happened at this time, according to Digger, was that the lights were too dim, and with all those candles shining in her face, the girl scout carrying the cake, couldn't see where she was going and lost her bearings, and she tripped over Lita Jean Jenson's foot which was there strictly for the cake and ice cream, as she didn't actually know the deceased, and dumped the cake and the candles into the casket with the corpse, which it caught the lining on fire, and by the time they got it out, it had completely burned the eyebrows and all the hair off Walter Broomhandle's head, and when his widow got a look at him, she said, well, he looks like a knockwurst right off the grill, and maybe you should just spread some mustard on him while you are at it, but as Digger said, they did not have any available, as it is not something that is generally called for in their line of work. So, they have suspended that particular option while they rethink it, especially the mustard part of it.

This year for the first time the Mortuary has a line of Holiday Selections, for those who care to combine their grieving with some good old fashioned family fun. As a for instance, the Memorial Day service includes a barbeque supper in the vestibule which includes Texas Brisket Delight, Digger's own secret recipe for Cemetery Cole Slaw and Corn on the Bone, all served on paper plates for the convenience of those who want to take supper into the chapel with them. "But we leave out the baked beans," as Digger explained, "because you remember what happened at your Aunt Minna's funeral a few years back."

The Fourth of July Service is the Twenty One Gun Salute, wherein everyone climaxes when the boys from the local Civil War Reenactment Group fire their guns, loaded with blanks, into the throng of mourners at the cemetery, which did have one little mishap the last occasion when one of the boys accidentally loaded real bullets into his rifle, but it was only a distant cousin that he winged and the family were sorry that she had come anyway as no one wanted her there, so it was not made much of except for the cousin, who was upset.

Before the firing, however, there is the appearance by The Red Rockettes Drill Team from the Mountain Valley Academy of Tap and Baton, which they form an honor guard to lead the casket from the hearse to the burial site, and which is quite moving, as I am assured, and that it was originally intended to finish with Laci Coleman, the head Rockette, doing a cartwheel across that hole in the ground, which he asked Digger what that was called and he said that he called it a hole in the ground, and he opined with a laugh that he hoped that I knew the difference between that and elsewise, but on the one occasion when this was tried, Laci misjudged the size of her cavity, which all agree could happen to anyone, and fell into the hole, and she was just climbing out when the deceased's great aunt Matilda arrived late who can't see much at all, and she saw her climbing and said, "Glory be, he is returned from the grave," and someone said, "can't you see that is a she in a majorette's outfit," and she said, "Well, I guess I know my own nephew, don't I?"

The *pièce de résistance* of the Sleep Well's available services is the I Am Walking into Heaven Crematory Service, of which The Reporter could only see part, as there were no cremations planned at the time of his visit, but what he saw peeked his interest indeed and he looks forward to coming back for a full performance.

The key to this service, as Digger explained it, is the new, full-sized doors to the crematory oven, which are cleverly designed to look like the Pearly Gates, and are covered with sequins so that they sparkle aplenty when the disco lights are shined on them.

Along with this goes the new casket stand, the Motor-Matic Rotating and Tilt-able Model, which can be lowered or raised and adjusted in numerous clever ways. "Say you have a family of Munchkins," as Digger explained, "You can lower the casket right to the floor and as soon as they have gone, raise it back up for the normal people," which The Reporter appreciates his sensitiveness of.

The most amazing feature of the Motor-Matic, however, is a series of switches and levers that allow you to wheel it to those full-sized Pearly Gate doors. At the push of a button, the deceased's left leg is lifted slightly and bent at the knee, while the Pearly Gates open slowly and majestically to the tune of John Denver's "Country Roads". At the very same time, an associate gently depresses a pedal at the head end of the casket, which slowly tilts the casket upward. When it is almost vertical, a spring-loaded lever behind the deceased's back pushes him gently forward. The effect as he leaves the casket with his one foot extended and his knee bent, gives the exact impression that he is stepping off on his own through the Pearly Gates and into paradise.

"I have never seen anything so moving," said Digger. "I wept genuine tears during the manufacturer's demonstration, and that was only with a plastic dummy. Just imagine what it would be like with a real live corpse."

The Reporter confesses himself eager to see a demonstration of this; Unfortunately, the only service scheduled for the weekend of his visit was the Mid Price special, which the widow, Angel Ashwell, had requested the Christmas theme, and Digger had said it might be a little early for that, and she said, well, K Mart has already got their Christmas display up, and he said, well, that is all right then, because if you can't trust K Mart, who can you trust? So the coffin was trimmed in those little multi-colored twinkle lights, and a plastic Santa stood on a special platform near the head of the casket, and the music was "Jingle Bells, Jingle Bells, Jingle Bell Rock", of which this reporter is quite fond while Santa twisted his hips around and around, which is sure to take your mind off things.

To be entirely honest, though, this service would have been skipped by The Reporter altogether except that The Friend and The Mother wanted to attend, as this was for Jeremiah Ashwell, and the Mother said she wanted to see for herself that the old goat got planted firmly, which is a term of affection that she sometimes uses, as it would be a relief to all and there would be quite a few women afterward without those ugly pinch-marks on their bottoms, which of course he had never pinched hers because he surely knew the difference between a lady and a tramp, and also The Motor Matic casket stand was being used, not because there was any cremating planned, but "Just to give our attendants some practice using it," as Digger explained, and The Reporter was eager to see how it performed.

Well, we had all taken our paper plates of baked ham, sweet potato casserole, and green beans into the chapel where the ceremony was to take place, as no one wanted to miss a minute of it because of the holiday aurora, and the family had just settled themselves in the front row of seats, and who should come in but Carol Louise Throckleberry, who everyone knew had been old Jeremiah's lady friend for ages, and she sashayed right up to the front of the room as bold as brass, and the widow, Angel Ashwell, licked the sweet potatoes off her fingers, as the Mortuary had forgotten to supply napkins, and said where did she think she was going, as these seats were reserved for the family, and Carol Louise said she wouldn't sit within half a mile of that bunch of dog's peckers if she could help it, but she guessed she had as much right as anybody to come and say her farewells to the only man she had ever loved, and Angel said he might have been the only one she ever loved but he had practically had to take a number and get in line with the bikers to get into her bedroom and kindly keep her hands off the man in the casket, as he did not belong to her.

Well, Carol Louise took umbrage and she said not only was she going to touch her Darling Sweet Potato, as she called him, which had nothing to do with the casserole served by the mortuary, but she was going to give full vent to her grief as well, and she proceeded to climb right up on top of him in that casket, which was already crowded enough with Jeremiah in it, as a three-hundred-pound man takes up a lot of casket space and Digger was out of the jumbo size.

The widow Angel was incensed by this brazenness, and she leapt up and ran at Carol Louise and climbed atop the casket too, and the two were pulling hair and clawing at one another something fierce, and the Friend and the Mother thought it would be sensible for them to get up and stand next to the combatants so they could get a closer look, and The Friend suddenly let out a squeal and said, "He is lifting his leg," which someone must have tripped that secret button, and The Mother said, "That always meant he was getting ready to pee, maybe someone should get one of those plastic cups, just in case he forgot to take care of that before he went."

So while she was distracted by the lifting leg, Angel finally got a good grip on Carol Louise's hair and pulled it right off of her, as it was only a wig after all, and with her hair gone Carol Louise looked like Mister Clean except for the different shade of lipstick and she got so worked up she shoved at her violently and she fell down across the foot of the casket, and she must have landed on the lifting pedal, only she landed with such force that, instead of the casket rising gently into the air as intended, it shot upward like a slingshot, and the corpse was violently ejected from the casket, "like that man they shoot out of a cannon at the county fair," as The Mother described it later, and he sailed bent leg and all right through the stained glass window of the chapel and thirty feet through the air, and landed smack dab atop Mrs. Fran Inwood and Miss May Charleston who were just emerging from the Good Buy Market and Car Wash across the way where they had done their weekly shopping, which seniors get ten percent off on Thursdays, and the ladies expressed their surprise indeed about being set upon by a corpse from above, though Miss Charleston said she thought at first it was her husband pulling another of his silly stunts, which was the kind of thing he liked to do to fool you.

"It was just like that movie, *The Night of the Living Dead*," Mrs. Inwood said, "except it was daylight, which is one of my favorites and I have seen it about twenty times, but it is scary, isn't it?"

Of course the paramedics were called immediately, and the first thing they did was to examine Jeremiah Ashwell, since he was the one who had sailed through the air, and the chief paramedic said, "This one is too far gone for our help, and it looks like he has lost his left leg."

Neither of the ladies suffered any serious damage, although Mrs. Inwood's eggs were crushed and Miss Charlestown said her milk was curdled, but the Reporter believes she was speaking symbolically.

Order was restored in due time, but Angel Ashwell said she was not going back inside and she was not going to pay for the service either until they found Jeremiah's missing leg, as he had two on him when he was brought in, and she didn't want to put him into the ground in installments, and the Mother mentioned casually that she had visited a very elegant home once where they had made an umbrella stand out of an elephant's foot, and maybe that was what had prompted someone to make off with the leg, although she thought it would not hold anything but one of those little purse-sized Totes if that was what was intended, since because Jeremiah's foot was plenty big enough but he had those scrawny little ankles, and if you cut them off you'd have nothing more than a pancake of an umbrella stand, which caused the widow Angel to express a new outpouring of grief at the thought of umbrellas in her husband's foot, regardless of what size.

Well, the rest of the service was suspended and Digger asked that those who hadn't finished their ham and sweet potatoes would kindly return them to the vestibule while authorities put out an alarm for someone with an extra leg, but personally The Mother said in an aside that she suspicions it was Carol Louise who had disappeared on the run while everyone was concentrated on the paramedics with something under her arm that might have been an appendage.

The Reporter feels that he can enthusiastically recommend the Sleep Well Mortuary to all of you who may have lost someone special or are just looking for a fun place to while away an afternoon or evening, as there is always something going on there, though you cannot count on seeing a corpse sail through a window just every day. Also, he is still eager to see that Motor Matic in proper action for a cremation.

In closing, Mister Digger has asked me to mention that they do taxidermy as well, which is an alternative for anyone who simply cannot bear the thought of parting with a loved one and would like to have them in the parlor where they can see them and talk to them over the years; and if any of you lose both a family member and a pet at the same time, they have a special two for one rate.

Until next time, this is The Underground Reporter saying, Happy Trails to You.

THE UNDERGROUND REPORTER COLUMN FOR NOVEMBER 5

"CHEAP IS OUR PROMISE": BLANCHE FERGUSON'S MAISON DE BEAUTÉ FOR MISSES AND MADAMS

NOVEMBER 4, 2005—This week the Underground Reporter paid a visit to a long established business establishment in our fair community, Blanche Ferguson's Maison de Beauté for Misses and Madams, or, as it is known to all the ladies locally, Blanche's, which everyone agrees is easier to say, though of course it is not so elegant as the Italian version.

The proprietress, who is Madam Blanche, told us that she has been in business at the same location for sixteen months, not counting the three months that it took her to clean up the mess left by the previous owners so that, as she put it succinctly, "you could step through the door without upchucking," which is a record, as none of the previous businesses at this location lasted more than six months.

The Reporter can state absolutely that he did not upchuck when stepping through the door of this friendly institution, though he does admit that the smells are unusual for a man who is not accustomed to the rigors of the beauty parlor, which in a man's barber shop smells mostly like Mennen's and Brylcreme, at least in the better class shops, as your average woman does not shave except for her legs and personal locations but not her face.

"Well, we do use a number of chemicals," Madam Blanche explained when he questioned her on this particular contre-temps. "There are all sorts of gels, and we use rinses, and there are the perm solutions, and that's just the beginning. You just can't go to work on a roomful of our local ladies in a beauty parlor without the place smelling some. And then there is the kerosene, which is for the lawnmower demonstration, but that's only here once a week."

Speaking of which, The Reporter asked her about the safety of these various chemicals, as you read about that sort of thing today, and especially the perm solutions, which there are some in particular who question if they are safe, and what do they do to a person's plumbing.

"Now, someone has been talking to Belinda Biddlinger," she said smartly, "and I am not permitted to get into that lawsuit business as I have been in his chambers with Judge Castorol and he gagged me repeatedly, but I will just say one thing, which is that everyone knows perfectly well that Belinda has been going bald for ages, I think it is something she eats, and aside from her and three or four others who have lost maybe just a hair or two each, we have never had a problem with our perms, regardless of what anyone might say. And we do dozens of color jobs every week, and except that Nancy Perkins hair came out purple, which I believe was something she ate, everyone has always been satisfied with their color, too, even when it wasn't what it started out to be, because sometimes a pleasant surprise can be nice."

Having said this, Madam Blanche gave notice of her opinion that The Reporter was showing a few gray hairs himself, which he usually keeps combed under so they don't show but the wind had shuffled them around, and she suggested that perhaps they could demonstrate for me by coloring my hair, and I said that was a good idea, so she seated me in one of the chairs between Audrey Mason who was getting rinsed with her Schnauzer dog, as the dog's name is Gourmet, which she pronounces

"Gour-may," because it is French although the dog is of a German descent, but which she calls Pom Pom because she was off gourmet cooking after a pancake accident that occurred to her of late, and Betty Sue Kowalski who was a perm, and I wouldn't do that if it wasn't safe, she told me,

"All of our colorists are thoroughly trained experts, as they study their chemicals at great length, for as long three days, some of the slower ones," Madam Blanche explained, and she set her assistant, Deanna Dendrige, who she attested was a genuine expert, to mixing the color formula for The Reporter's hair which she described as Autumn Foliage Brown, while she tied an enormous napkin around his neck in case he dripped.

Also performed next was, his head was dipped into a sink so it could be shampooed, so that the color wouldn't be conflicted with any hair gel or such, although The Reporter informed her that he uses nothing but spit when he combs his hair, which Madam Blanche said, well, spit can have all kinds of things in it, and there is no telling what, say, a salami sandwich for lunch if you had one, (although The Reporter had tuna salad on rye with no seeds), would do to Autumn Foliage Brown, and it was better to be safe than sorry, as you wouldn't want your head looking funny, although she added, in your case I suppose people are used to it, and she laughed capriciously to show that she was only being jocular, and The Reporter would have laughed too except that his head was underwater washing out that salami sandwich which he hadn't had anyway, but there is little doubt the tuna went too.

Once it had been toweled dry, the color formula was applied to his hair which Deanna Dendrige had formulated, and it was allowed to set for a bit, "to take hold," as it was explained, which was the hard part as, despite all Madam Blanche's assurances, Betty Sue Kowalski had the aroma of rotten eggs, which he made the assumption that it was her perm, as it did not seem likely she would choose a perfume like that, though Audrey Mason wasn't noticeable except for a nose that kept investigating my private lap regions, which was her dog, Gourmet, who she calls Pom Pom, because as she explained it he had recently burned his mouth.

While we waited, Madam Blanche explained to me about her shop's "daily specials," which were various kinds of divertissements that she had arranged for her customers, "as it can get tedious just sitting there, especially if it is too early for the soaps."

Normally, as she explained, this being Friday, they would have representatives from the Mountain Valley Academy of Tap and Baton, to demonstrate their twirling, which is one of our local cultural treasures, as she expressed it. "When I was a girl," she said, "If you had any pretensions to culture, you took tap or baton, but young ladies today are not so refined, in my opinion."

However, a little accident had been suffered by Laci Coleman, who was to have entertained us, which is a delight as The Reporter well knows, having been delightfully entertained a time or two in the past by her, as she misjudged a cavity at the cemetery while participating in a service, and now has a bandaged ankle which gets in her way.

On Saturdays, The Fancy Cook, who used to be Peter Childless, normally comes in to give a cooking demonstration, and this weekend was to be a demonstration of chicken bosoms, which he says without nipples they cannot properly be called breasts, and he had never seen a chicken that had any, "but he recently discovered that he was a woman in a man's body," as Madam Blanche explained it, "and so he is busy changing into Tulia Childless which he says he is more comfortable, though he does not as yet have any breasts, which he says cannot be called bosoms, as he does have nipples but as we sometimes have children they cannot be shown here in the shop.

"Sundays and Mondays are closed, and on Tuesdays the choir from the West Pentecostal Church comes to sing with Zoe Pickerwell as soloist and their rendition of 'Jesus Wants Me for a Sunbeam' would bring tears to anyone's eyes, in my opinion, which The Reporter can certainly understand, having heard Zoe sing.

"Wednesday is pet day, and you can have your pet rinsed and groomed right alongside your own head, and even tinted or permed if you like, although it is hard to get them to sit still for the curlers, which Audrey had planned for her Pom Pom, except she got her days confused and since she was here I said we might as well go ahead and do something with her hair, as it was looking pitiful, which she says she cannot get a good night's sleep after having been assaulted by Vanda Pomeroy in the boy's shower at the high school, which was a misunderstanding, and Vanda's leg has now healed, but she is no longer friendly with Audrey and I have to schedule their appointments for different days because she says she won't sit next to anyone who bites her shin," which The Reporter can certainly agree with that stipulation.

"Then on Thursdays," Blanche embellished, "The school crossing guards do their drill routine for us after the children have all crossed the street, and we get a lecture on a timely subject, such as crossing safely or how to watch out for drivers who are reckless or careless, as we all know they are out there and some of them just seem to try to run you down, because of their cell phones. Plus, Sam Kelly from the tractor store comes in to demonstrate starting a lawnmower and he puts down an old rug to be the grass and cuts a patch of it for us, so we will know what to do."

Well, as you can see from the above, dear readers, there is always something afoot at the Madam's, and I for one plan to make a point of regular visits even when my hair doesn't need anything.

Which, The Reporter regrets that he has to say, it will, since the Autumn Foliage Brown didn't come out right. "It doesn't look exactly like the box," Madam Blanche alluded to me before handing me a mirror to see for myself, which The Reporter agrees with, as the box showed a handsome young man with a full head of curly dark brown hair, and The Reporter had something atop his head that looked like frizzy green pea soup although he had not expected to come out looking like the handsome young man, which some people say in all modesty that he isn't so bad, however, but that is without the pea soup.

Well, in all sagacity, The Reporter did not feel that he wanted to go about the rest of his day looking as he did even without the blackface which came about later, although Betty Sue Kowalski made the reference that the hair color was exactly the color she had been looking to find for her dining room and they just hadn't come even close with the chips at the paint store and would The Reporter mind stopping by with her only she had to wait for her perm to finish, and The Reporter noticed that little Pom Pom the Schnauzer had even lost interest in his lap privates because as Audrey said, "he was once frightened by a can of peas and you can't get him to go near one since then," which The Reporter was glad to be free of that nose by whatever name.

Unfortunately, The Reporter thought it probably the best wisdom to go ahead and see what we could do with it for the present, which he was not comfortable in a paint store with pea soup hair, though he would have liked to help Betty Sue over, and that was probably a mistake, as Deanna Dendrige, who had mixed up the hair color that was supposed to be Autumn Foliage Brown was now nervous, and as she explained later, "when I get my nerves suffered, my stomach goes all out of whack, and I just can't think what I am doing to save my soul."

Which when she tried to mix up another batch, her stomach got her all confused, and Madam Blanche said later she would have made up the second batch herself but it was time to get that perm off of Betty Sue, because the hair can fall out after too long, and Audrey had just had her hair rinsed in the sink, which she said came out exactly the color she had been hoping for, except she hadn't expected it to turn curly the way it had, and Deanna Dendrige poured something from one bottle into a bottle of something else, and there was this giant explosion, and clouds of black smoke, and Madam Blanche expressed the opinion later that things wouldn't have been half bad if Audrey hadn't lost her presence of mind and grabbed what she thought was a bucket of water which was really the kerosene, which she said it was because of her curly hair, which was on her mind.

When the firemen saw The Reporter they said they had never seen a man in black face with pea soup on the top of his head standing on an ordinary street, as he had chosen to leave the premises until the fire was contained, which even the smoke hadn't changed the color of that hair, only Betty Sue was now bald, as the perm solution must have caught on fire along with the shop, and Audrey's hair was now black and blue, and she kept yelling for the firemen that she couldn't find her Pom Pom and did anybody know what had happened to her Pom Pom and the fire chief said if it wasn't covered up and it was close to that fire, her Pom Pom was probably burned bald the same as Betty Sue's scalp, and that was probably why she didn't recognize it, and it wasn't until they took the hose up to the roof because the buildings on either side had caught fire too, being Teensy Anna's, which is a children's specialty store, and The Quacked Duck which is a bar on the other side, that they found him where he had been blown clear through the ceiling and he was bald too, and The Reporter thought that all in all a man with pea soup hair was probably not as funny looking as a bald Schnauzer who is black all over, which Audrey was not amused by, but her nerves have been shattered since that business with Vanda Pomeroy which left her with not much sense of humor.

The Reporter recommends Blanche Ferguson's Maison de Beauté for Misses and Madams, except it will be a few weeks before the fire damage is repaired, and he does say you may want to stay away from Autumn Foliage Brown when picking a color, but you can take a look at Betty Sue Kowalski's dining room if you are uncertain, as she informs me that she found the paint she wanted and for which she is grateful to The Reporter. Also, you might want to think twice about taking your dog with you, as little Pom Pom has yet to start growing his hair back, and a bald Schnauzer is a peculiar looking creature even with the black scrubbed off.

THE MARAUDING CHICKEN: HEADLINE, *WALTONSBERG WEST PANHANDLE EXPRESS*, JULY 22, 2006

MARAUDING CHICKEN ACQUITTED

"Our family is reunited"

While her fans and supporters rallied and cheered outside the Waltonsberg Court House today, Judge Helen Bonami acquitted Candice, the hen, of all charges of highway impairment, and the happy Rhode Island Red was allowed to leave with her relieved family.

Candice was cited June 14 when she was discovered by the West Virginia Highway Patrol on Interstate 80 just north of Waltonsberg, where she had somehow managed to assemble a nest in the northbound lane, upon which she was roosting, and her familial ministrations had created a two mile backup as drivers waited patiently for her eggs to hatch. "And who knows when that would have been," said Jason Cartwheel of Outfarm, one of several delayed drivers who had set up a pinochle game on his shoulder to pass the time.

Candice's attorney, James Faulkner, argued successfully that the law cited pertained to livestock on the highway, as a for instance, cows, which all could agree that a cow nesting on the highway would be a real hazard, and specifically excluded domestic pets.

"Oh, my yes, she is a domestic pet," Candice's mistress, Rose Bunyan, told the Express when questioned. "Why, she even sleeps in the bed with me when Fred works the night shift. You do have that egg thing to look out for, which can be uncomfortable at three in the morning, and I have scolded her for that, which is no doubt what drove the poor little thing onto the interstate. I think her maternal clock was just ticking something fierce and I blame myself for it. As far as sharing a bed with her, however, there is one thing in her favor: you don't have that gas business that I get with Fred or the Bassett either one. I have a Barbie peignoir which she wears, and I always give her a generous dressing of night cream before we retire, which I believe is one of the reasons she still looks like a young chick, unlike her siblings.

"Candice is very much the one for dressing for the occasion, too. When we have company in for poker, she loves to wear her little Barbie costumes. I'm sure everyone noticed the pillbox hat with the dark veil that she wore on the witness stand, which we thought more suitable to the occasion, but for festive times she wears the wide brimmed hat with the bitty cabbage roses, which we have to hold in place with a bit of ribbon under her beak, and she is particularly fond of the tiny heart pendant, which she wears so proudly on her henly bosom. Her favorite outfit is the tropical shift in watermelon red with green and white sunbursts, which sets off her coloration very nicely, I think, and with that she likes to wear the open-toed platform shoes, though she does have a bit of trouble balancing on them, as they were not designed for ladies of the three-toed sort, particularly after she has had a beer or two with our guests, as she likes to be sociable, and often this finds her on her back with her legs in the air—"just like someone down the block," as Mother says, "but I am not going to name any names."

Friends and supporters plan a victory celebration at the Lucky Pierre Dining Room at the Happy Deuce Motel, with a no host bar, and those who wish to join in the festivities are invited to bring along a covered dish, anything you like, except, no stuffed eggs, please.

AFTERWORD

Someone once complained of me that I was out of touch with reality. Harrumph. I am quite fond of reality, actually; I am just not convinced that this is it.

Many years ago, I took one of those self-help tests that you find in women's magazines—this may have been in *Cosmopolitan*, I'm not sure now—and according to my score, I was just plain crazy.

There are certainly worse things, in my opinion. Bad breath makes socializing difficult, and you can't get much pleasure out of shopping with bad feet, and bad manners are so dreadful that I won't even get into that subject, except to point out that in every great civilization that has come and gone on our planet, the first indication of the decay of that culture was a decline in everyday manners, which says something, I think, about our obsession today with road rage and cell phone use.

To be honest, though, crazy didn't seem all that calamitous to me. I did give some thought to the options. I could just have myself committed, but when I thought about the places where I would then spend my time, it did seem to me that most of them were utterly dreary. Suicide was presumably an option, but that meant I never would master making a Baked Alaska, a dessert which, at that time, I had been struggling with for ages without success, though I have since come to think that it isn't all that special anyway. I think it was mostly the challenge that intrigued me.

Which left me, the way I saw it, with only one sensible option, and that was just to get on with it, which is what I opted to do. I accepted without rancor that I was never going to be anything that anyone would call normal, and I said goodbye to that possibility with little regret. There is one true blessing in being crazy, and that is, the stuff that most people stew over ends up striking you as funny; so you trade much of what others settle happily for, for a lot of laughs. I have never thought that was such a bad trade-off, and I have more than once told friends and family that if the day comes when I stop laughing, it's time to start digging that hole in the back yard, as it will then be all over as far as I am concerned.

I have written upon some serious matters in this collection, but also upon some very silly matters, and in a silly fashion upon some of the serious ones. I hope I have not offended too many readers, but it does not perturb me in the least to think that I may have offended some, and if you are too adamant in your objections, I am sorry to tell you it is probably only going to give me one more thing to laugh about, and there is simply nothing that either of us can do to change that.

John Gay put it so neatly, "Life is a Jest, and all things show it; I thought so once, and now I know it." The fact that I laugh at so many things, or perhaps I should say, that I see the joke in so many things, does not mean, however, that I think of either life or writing as trivial or silly; quite the opposite.

We live in a world today in which the arts are too often looked upon as something frou-frou, optional at extra cost, like special tinted windows on a new car. When schools and cities cut their budgets, the first programs to be slashed are too often those dealing with the arts.

I think that is funny, but it is also quite sad. We, the artists, have an ancient lineage; we go back as far as mankind goes back. In my crazy mind's eye, I see a small group, in strikingly designed animal skin costumes, gathered about a fire in a smartly decorated but somewhat smoky cave. Outside, some fearsome beast, perhaps a saber toothed tiger, roars, and everyone is sensibly frightened.

To distract himself and the others, silly Victor, who has just returned from a shopping trip which took him over some distant hills, because they never have what I am looking for in my neighborhood stores, begins to tell them a story of a herd of bison—or they may have been buffalo, it is hard to tell them apart—that he saw on the other side of the valley. Todd, who had been shopping with him, jumps up and begins to sketch the bison—or perhaps buffalo—on the wall of the cave, although anyone who knows Todd will know that his sketches were crude and didn't do the animals justice.

When Victor reaches the point in his story where a crash of thunder startles the bison—or buffalo—and they begin to stampede down the hillside, Jake is inspired to play the rhythm of their hoof beats on a hollow log; and Lynette is so delighted with his drumming that she leaps to her feet and begins to dance around the campfire.

What I am trying to say is that we are a fundamental part of what makes us mankind, of what separates us from the animals. We go back to the very beginning, and we, the storyteller, the musician, the painter, the dancer, the actor, *et alii*, are the custodians of the most ancient of all the temples of humankind: Art. And of all the arts, the art of storytelling is, of course, the first and the one from which all the others spring.

I don't know what could be more serious or more sacred than that.

I just happen to find it often funny, is all; but, admittedly, I am crazy.

ACKNOWLEDGMENTS

"Welcome to Antoinette's" was first published in *The Main ARTery*, Volume 1, Issue 5, and is reprinted here with permission of the publisher.

"The Mushroom King" is excerpted from *Spine Intact, Some Creases*, by Victor J. Banis; ECIG, 2005; Borgo Press, 2007.

"Anne's Wedding Night" is excerpted from *This Splendid Earth*, St. Martin's Press, 1978; Borgo Press, 2007.

"In a Small Town" is excerpted from *Spine Intact, Some Creases*, ECIG, 2005; Borgo Press, 2007.

"Loaves and Fishes" was first published in *The Main ARTery*, Volume 1, Issue 1, and is reprinted here with permission of the publisher.

"The Master's Spell" is excerpted from the novel, *The Glass Painting*, Popular Library, 1972; Borgo Press, 2007.

ABOUT THE AUTHOR

V. J. BANIS is the critically acclaimed author ("the master's touch in storytelling..."—*Publishers Weekly*) of more than 150 published books and numerous short stories in a career spanning nearly a half century. A native of Ohio and a longtime Californian, he lives and writes now in West Virginia's beautiful Blue Ridge.

You can visit him at http://www.vjbanis.com